The Change^{16}

Insights into Self-Empowerment

Jim Britt ~ Jim Lutes

With

Co-authors from Around the World

The Change[16]

Jim Britt ~ Jim Lutes

All Rights Reserved

Copyright 2017

The Change

10556 Combie Road, Suite 6205

Auburn, CA 95602

The use of any part of this publication, whether reproduced, stored in any retrieval system, or transmitted in any forms or by any means, electronic or otherwise, without the prior written consent of the publisher, is an infringement of copyright law.

Jim Lutes ~ Jim Britt

Text Setting: ZONOikO

The Change[16]

ISBN: 978-1-63227-262-1

Co-authors

Dr. Spencer J. Holman

Christine Suva

Craig Wayne Boyd

Bill Holmes

Russell Reich

Merrilee Sweeney

Phil Bristol

Stacey Cargnelutti

Mike Greenly & Bill Holmes

Erin McDonnell

Jimmy Star

Jeff Metz

David Norris

Josephine H. Wilcox

Dr. Tianna Conte and Rev. Azima Jackson

Pamela Church

Venetia Zannettis

Michelle Gesky

Asha Mankowska

Mark Recker

The Change is proud to support Good Women International.

Every five minutes, one American child (many as young as ten years old) will be abducted and trafficked into the sex trade. 274 children a day, 100,000 each year and that estimate could be low. The total current number of human trafficking victims in the U.S. alone reaches into the hundreds of thousands and worldwide into the millions.

All profits from the sale of Amazon Kindle electronic books are being donated to Good Women International, whose focus is on the prevention of sexual exploitation of young women and children. They support self-empowerment and educational programs worldwide designed to educate our youth to avoid becoming a victim. A recent successful project was an anti-trafficking curricula for our high schools which is now complete and being utilized in many high schools around the world.

Enslavement is a reality. It is documented and it is real. The question is: What are we going to do about it?

To make a donation to Good Women International, a non-profit subsidiary of Village Care International, go to: www.SupportGoodWomen.com. All donations are tax deductible under Tax ID #: 88-0471768. We welcome and appreciate your donations, no matter how small.

http://GoodWomenInternational.org

Note: Donations are never for salaries, as Good Women is a volunteer organization.

DEDICATION

This book is dedicated to all those seeking change

Foreword

By Les Brown

Many of us spend at least a good part of our day going over internal dialog. We relive past experiences, worry about the future, blame the outside world for our shortcomings and criticize ourselves for not having all we want by this point in our lives. We do this both consciously and unconsciously. Even while we are listening to others we aren't really fully present. Instead we are rehearsing our answers, slipping back into yesterday and worrying about tomorrow.

We live in uncertain times. We all feel we have minimum control over being able to change external circumstances, but we do have control over being able to change our internal environment, not only being able to see the truth behind a given situation but also how we respond to it. And to get the best out of the most stressful times, we need to demand the best from ourselves.

Many feel the pain of unhappiness. So many suffer from it daily, unaware that they can eliminate their suffering and find happiness by simply seeing the truth behind their unhappiness and making the right choices to change it. The problem is that our emotional conflicts are so familiar to us that they keep us blinded to better possibilities. We actually become addicted to feeling the way we do, thinking that it is just the way things are and we resign ourselves to getting by and coping.

I have had the privilege of speaking for over forty years serving millions of people from over 51 different countries. I know that there are certain patterns that create success and other patterns that breed internal conflict and failures.

The secret to being fulfilled and living the life you want is having the courage to go beyond the skills you've learned and discover the gifts that you were born with and to implement them daily. So many people settle for less in life, but I can tell you from my experience that it doesn't have to be that way.

I was born in an abandoned building on a floor with a twin brother in a poor section in Miami Florida called Liberty City. When we were six weeks of age we were adopted by Mrs. Mimi Brown. Whenever I speak I always say that all that I am and all I ever hope to be I owe to my mother.

When I was in the fifth grade I was labeled educable mentally retarded and put back from the fifth grade to the fourth grade and failed again when I was in the eighth grade. Mrs. Mimi Brown took my brother and I and five other kids in as foster kids and eventually adopted us.

Because of the work that Jim Britt does and the methods and techniques he uses to change your story and how you see yourself, it enabled me to build my career to make it against all odds. Both Jim Britt and Jim Lutes are icons in personal development and empowering others to be the best they can be.

You have something special inside. You have greatness in you. When you read this book it will take you on a journey and introduce you to a part of yourself that has remained hidden and you didn't know existed.

When you begin to look at your goals and dreams realize that you have greatness inside you. The Change will provide the insights and processes of self-development that will empower you to manifest your greatness.

Jim Britt and I actually started the foundation of our speaking careers in the same direct selling company, Bestline, over 40 years ago. Although I haven't followed Jim Britt's career over the years, but I do know that he is recognized as one of the top thought leaders in the world, helping millions of people create prosperous lives, rewarding relationships and spiritual awareness. He has authored 13 books and multiple programs showing people how to understand their hidden abilities to do more, become more and enjoy more in every area of life.

Today, Jim Britt and mind programming expert, Jim Lutes, along with inspiring co-authors from around the world, bring a pioneering work "The Change" book series to the market to transform lives. Their principles are forged on touching millions on every continent. As you read, you are exploring self-empowerment principles from a whole different perspective. In fact, Jim and Jim's publications of The Change book series now has hundreds of coauthors in 26 countries. The real power in each book is that 20 coauthors share their inspiring story so that the reader may benefit from their experience. It is packed with life-changing ideas, stories, tips, strategies on various empowering topics that you will love.

The principles, concepts and ideas within this book are sometimes simple, but can be profound to a person who is ready for that perfect message at the right time and is willing to take action to change. Maybe for one it's a chapter on relationships or leadership. For the next maybe it's a chapter on forgiveness or health awareness, and for another a simple life-changing message like I received as a youngster from a teacher. Each chapter is like opening a surprise empowering gift.

As I travel the world presenting my seminars I meet people who spend more time and energy focused on what's wrong with society and their lives than is spent on helping each other improve the quality of life. With so much time spent on social media we often fear intimate contact with each other. Mistrust is often our first reaction. We judge and sometimes brutalize those among us who are in any way different from ourselves. We become addicted to anything that allows us a brief consolidation from the terrible pain we feel inside.

We need to begin to understand more about ourselves and our condition if there is ever to be the possibility of a healthy society. I believe this is possible and that's why I am so passionate about the work I do. Simply put…we are at war with ourselves. Real healing only takes place when we are willing to experience and face the truth within.

The conclusion to me is an exciting one. You, me and every other human being are shaping our brains and bodies by the thoughts we think, the emotions we feel, the intentions we hold, and the actions we take daily. Why is it exciting? Because we are in control of all these things and we can change as long as we have the intention, willingness and commitment to look inside, take charge of our lives and make the changes.

Whether you're pursuing, your dreams as an entrepreneur, a business owner or you want a more fulfilling relationship, or simply want to live a happy life, being authentic and actively appreciating what you're really capable of is going to be one of the most important assets you possess. It will make the difference between just "getting by" and really thriving and experiencing happiness or internal conflict.

Self-knowledge provides you the emotional edge that will help you create a better life not only for yourself, but also for everyone with whom yo;u come in contact.

This is the time to extract the best out of yourself and to use that gift to touch the lives of others.

I want to congratulate Jim Britt and Jim Lutes for making this publication series available and for allowing me to write the foreword. I honor them both and the coauthors within this book and the series for the lives they are changing.

As you enter these pages, do so slowly and with an open mind. Savor the wisdom you discover here, and then with interest and curiosity discover what rings true for you, and then take action toward the life you want.

Be prepared…because your life is about to change.

Hope to meet you one day at one of my seminars. And remember, everything you do counts!

Les Brown

Table of Contents

Foreword vi

Jim Britt: The Predator and the Prey 1

Jim Lutes: It's Not Where You Are, It's Where You're Going .. 13

Dr Spencer J. Holman: The 10 Life Values: An Examined Life! 21

Christine Suva: Mastering Your Mindset for Success! 33

Craig Wayne Boyd: I'm Still Here 45

Bill Holmes: How I Learned : the Value of "Adjusting" 57

Russell Reich: How to Get Any Job You Want 67

Merrilee Sweeney: The Problem with Women 79

Phil Bristol: Don't Let the Family Drama Vortex Shatter Your Family Business Legacy 89

Stacey Cargnelutti: From Faith to Fitness 103

Mike Greenly & Bill Holmes: The Power of Paying Attention 115

Erin McDonnell: Overcoming Eating Disorders & Depression 127

Jimmy Star: Secrets of Social Media Success 139

Jeff Metz: People First – Always! 149

David Norris: IS IT GOOD TO BE YOU? 159

Josephine H. Wilcox: Broken to Butterfly 169

Dr. Tianna Conte and Rev. Azima Jackson: Extraordinary Journey 175

Pamela Church: Financial Shift 189

Venetia Zannettis: Stepping Out of Denial into My Truth 199

Michelle Gesky: The "Sh#*%" Word 209

Asha Mankowska: Manifest Your Greatness Today 219

Mark Recker: Biography of Entrepreneur Mark Recker 231

Afterword 231

Jim Britt

Jim Britt is an internationally recognized leader in the field of peak performance and personal empowerment training. He is author of 13 best-selling books, including *Cracking the Rich Code; Cracking the Life Code; Rings of Truth; The Power of Letting Go; Freedom; Unleashing Your Authentic Power; Do This. Get Rich-For Entrepreneurs; The Flaw in The Law of Attraction;* and *The Law of Realization,* to name a few.

Jim has presented seminars throughout the world sharing his success principles and life-enhancing realizations with thousands of audiences, totaling over 1,000,000 people from all walks of life.

Jim has served as a success counselor to over 300 corporations worldwide. He was recently named as one of the world's top 20 success coaches and presented with the best of the best award out of the top 100 contributors of all time to the direct selling industry.

Jim is more than aware of the challenges we all face in making adaptive changes for a sustainable future.

The Predator and the Prey

By Jim Britt

Maybe you have dreams and goals, but somehow things are simply not moving in the direction you had planned? Or worse, maybe you've stopped believing that the life you've always wanted is even attainable?

Let me ask you. Do you see similarities between you and your parents? The reality is that DNA passes down through generations… you, your parents, grandparents, great-grandparents, and so on. You could actually track it right back to when your ancestors lived in a cave. And in order to survive, prehistoric man needed to be able to see an event and interpret it as danger or safe…immediately! They had two dominant thoughts, "kill something to eat" and "keep from being killed and eaten." And to some degree, we still have this mechanism of recognition in place today. We just don't view it the same way.

Something happens… and your brain stretches and searches all through your past networks… or dendrites, which are the memory channels woven throughout your DNA looking to match some sort of pattern so you can make an instant decision… is this safe or dangerous? The meaning you give something is based upon a constant comparison of your past experiences and DNA programming projected into the future with the anticipation or possibility of it happening again. Something happens and you immediately tell yourself a story about what it means. Remember, it's a made-up story in your mind. It's not real… yet.

So when you step into the future, you don't really step into an empty future, but rather into a future that is filled with interpretations about what happened in the past, and what could happen in the future if you proceed.

For example, a salesperson prepares her presentation. She is excited for that important appointment to make a sale, but instead of a sale she gets a very rude "no." Now the next presentation, she won't step into a blank future, but rather, first, she steps into a previous negative past experience. Put enough of these "no's" together and now the salesperson does everything in her power to avoid prospecting so she doesn't have to experience another 'no.' Again, the rejection had no meaning until she gave it one. She got a "no" and she made it mean something about her, when in reality it wasn't about her at all.

Imagine three circles. A circle on the left. In that circle something happens to you... broken marriage, lose money in a business venture. You decide what goes in there.

Now there's the circle on the right. This is where you gave what happened to you meaning. Examples...bad experience with last business. Business didn't work last time and may not work now. Marriage ended in divorce. I don't want that again. You gave whatever happened to you a meaning.

Now, the circle on bottom. You live your life as if your story is true. We live in a black and white world.

However, most live their life in the gray as if their story is true, when in reality, it's a made-up story created from past experiences. This is an example of inauthentic living. You are living as if your story is true and reacting accordingly. Everyone has a story, but the reality is that your story is in large part an illusion... it's a made-up belief. All beliefs are false until you decide they are true, but that doesn't make them true. But if you decide it is true, then it will be true for you.

Core beliefs work like sunglasses. Sunglasses change incoming light before it hits our eyes. The world does not change to a shaded image just because you put on sunglasses. Only your perception changes looking through the glasses. Wear sunglasses long enough and you will eventually forget you have them on.

That's how beliefs work as well. Believe something long enough and eventually you experience it as true. It then becomes a core belief. Core beliefs change how you see the world before you are even aware of seeing anything. And core beliefs also determine how the world sees you. That's right. The world sees you the way you see you.

On the other hand, this mechanism is critical for your survival because it separates things that might get you killed and eaten from everything else. In a sense, your core beliefs protect you. But not always, because you automatically filter everything that happens to you according to core beliefs, which may or may not be true. In other words, your core beliefs may not be taking you in the direction you want to go.

Prey animals cannot afford to not follow their core beliefs. Humans are no exception. The top priority our brains have is to keep us from getting killed and eaten…maybe not literally in today's world. But, you may fear getting killed and eaten by an audience when you step on a stage, or by a prospect when making a presentation.

These things represent predators waiting to invade your refuge and attack you if you leave yourself open, or you start to take a risk. Our brains are wired to fear monsters, noises, and dangerous situations, because that is what our ancestors had to do to survive.

Humans of all ages establish and stick to routines no matter what, so they can survive. We take comfort in our routines. This makes perfect sense.

For example, if a predator attacks at dusk, then its prey should be out and about during the day and asleep and out of reach at night. If a predator attacks at noon, then the prey would most likely be nocturnal. Sticking to this routine helps the prey stay alive. Our prey habits are all about avoiding predators, discomfort, or dangerous situations.

Humans are prey animals whose top priority is not getting killed and eaten, avoiding pain, or not getting hurt. We therefore form habits to help us survive and then stick to those habits no matter how inconvenient, uncomfortable, unrealistic, or awful they are. We learned over countless generations that straying from our routine puts us at risk. Our brain does everything in its power to keep that from happening. This is why people refuse to change until the pain of *not* changing is worse than the pain of changing.

We desire to change, but when faced with the pain of change we weigh out both sides—the pain of staying where we are and the pain associated with changing. Whatever causes us less pain is what wins out. But the question is, do you win, or do you continue living a life of more of the same?

Core beliefs form our entire reality from birth to death unless we take action to change them. The good news is that you can change your beliefs. We do it all the time. Remember, a belief is a made-up story. Want to change it, make up something new!

It's like earning a six-figure income for example. Once you hit it, it becomes a core belief, so you settle for nothing less. The catch is that changing your beliefs will force you to confront programming that your brain interprets as being essential for your very survival. This is why crash diets, New Year's resolutions, joining a gym, opening a savings account, cutting up the credit cards, and other drastic changes rarely last more than a few days to a few weeks. At some point, the desire for change surrenders to the brain's built-in attempts to keep you from getting killed and eaten.

How do you change a core belief? Make up something new, let go of all that doesn't support it, and stick to it until it becomes a core belief.

Remember, every life level requires a different you. Think about that…EVERY LIFE LEVEL REQUIRES A DIFFERENT YOU.

The Change[16]

Just look at your own life. What are some examples of drastic changes you have attempted in your own life?

Change requires that you change your perceptions.

Imagine a gopher that hides from hungry birds during the day. Most gophers will not leave their burrows during the day unless some emergency happens. For example, flooding the burrow gives the gopher the choice of *certain* death by drowning or *possible* death by escaping. In this example, the risk of following the normal routine becomes greater than the risk of doing something different.

Humans work the same way, except that our fears are based on past experiences combined with future anticipations. These fears are not real. They are imagined. They are a made-up story based on past experiences and programming that are designed to keep us safe. Just like the gopher, we weigh out the pain of staying where we are, not taking a risk, staying where we are comfortable, versus doing something in a different way.

Our routines form what's known as our comfort zone. We refer to doing things we don't normally do as "leaving the comfort zone." How did you feel the last time you left your comfort zone? Maybe someone asked you to deliver a short speech to a group of your peers. You may have felt scared, nervous, insecure, and ready to bolt at a moment's notice. This is a perfect example of our prey instincts telling us to get back in our comfort zone as quickly as possible.

I remember my first experience speaking. I literally thought I would be killed and eaten! I was to speak for 20 minutes to a group of about 20 people. I prepared for a month. I must have written 20 pages of notes. I couldn't stop thinking about it. What might happen if I didn't do it right, or forgot what I was supposed to say, or I might say it wrong, make a mistake…the list was endless.

I was staying in a hotel the night before I was to speak. I couldn't sleep, for fear of being killed and eaten! I tried to think of ways I could get out of speaking. Nothing seemed to make any sense. Then

I came up with the answer. I will have an accident on the way to the speaking engagement. Not a huge one. Just something small, but big enough that I could show my bent fender so it looked legit. I figured the accident would be less painful than speaking.

Just as I went for the door to leave for my accident, someone knocked. I thought it was probably housekeeping, so I opened the door. It wasn't housekeeping. It was my associate that had booked the speaking engagement for me. He said, "I came to pick you up." My first thought was "you are going to be in an accident."

I said, "I'll drive."

He said, "No I'll drive."

I said, "No I want to drive."

He said, "I'm parked in front of the door. I'm driving."

I thought, "Do I grab the wheel of his car and have an accident?" I decided not to do that, but to follow through with the speech.

We arrived. I felt like I wanted to throw up. I was terrified. I took a few deep breaths and started my talk. I spoke for 20 minutes and I have no idea what I said. When I finished, I immediately went outside and stood beside the car and did a lot of deep breathing to regain my composure.

"Never again" was what I was thinking. After a few moments, I thought, "I have one of two choices. Never do it again, or do it often until I got better at it." After a lot of mental back and forth, I chose the latter.

I was in charge of about 300 salespeople that did presentations for small to medium sized groups to sell seminar tickets for a Jim Rohn seminar. I put the word out that I was available to do up to three presentations a day to groups of fifty or more…which I did for the next five years. And after about 15 presentations a week, almost 3500 total, I finally lost my fear of being killed and eaten by an audience. I created a new belief, a program that was stronger that the old one.

The stronger the urge to get back to your comfort zone increases, the farther you stray. This happens because our brains are wired to learn and follow habits designed to keep us safe and alive. We do this by learning how our predators behave and then creating patterns to avoid them, even if our predators only exist in our imagination. Like the "no" that the salesperson gets over and over, until now they are afraid to even prospect. The "no" becomes the predator.

Like the person that has been hurt multiple times in a relationship. And now the thought of getting involved in another relationship becomes very scary.

The comfort zone is nothing more or less than behavioral boundaries set by your core beliefs that were either formed when you were too young to understand what was happening, or over a long period of time through repeated experiences.

Core beliefs form your entire reality from birth to death unless you take action to change them. The good news is that you can change your beliefs. We do it all the time. Just think of something you used to believe that you no longer believe. Do you still believe what you believed in high school? Once you got out into the real world, you most likely looked back and laughed at some of the stupid things you did and what you believed to be true and realized it wasn't true at all.

It's like earning a six-figure income for example. Once you hit it, if that's the case, now you believe you can, so you settle for nothing less. That's called creating a new belief. The catch is that changing your beliefs will force you to confront programming that your brain interprets as being essential for your very survival.

Again, this is why crash diets, New Year's resolutions, joining a gym, opening a savings account, cutting up the credit cards, and other drastic changes rarely last more than a few days to a few weeks. At some point, the desire for change surrenders to the brain's built-in attempts to keep you from getting killed and eaten, unless you decide and commit to experiencing the pain of change and you stick with it until you change.

Just look at your own life. What are some examples of drastic changes you have attempted in your own life? How have they worked out for you?

How can you change when you run up against instincts designed to keep you safe and alive? A prey animal needs to react to predators without question. And if you want change, you have to become self-observant to determine what you should act upon and what is old programming that no longer serves your greater good.

Indecision causes hesitation. And if you hesitate, you could get killed and eaten! Hesitation gives predators an extra split second to move in for the kill.

It's starts with a decision to change whatever it is you want to change. So when one of those old programs arise, stop! Stop like you approach a red light at a busy intersection with a sign that reads "right turn on red after stop." Stop and ask yourself. "If I proceed, will this take me in the direction I want to go? Is this fear real or in my imagination, based on old programming?"

Take a good look at any animal whose parents raise the young. The young stick around to learn the survival skills they need to stay alive. Prey animals learn when they can come out, where to go, how to avoid predators, and when to retreat back home. Their survival depends on absorbing this information and mastering the skills without question. We were taught similar things. "That's hot, don't touch that, you'll go blind." "Careful, you'll fall."

Of course certain things we have learned have become essential to our survival. But unlike prey animals, we humans are programming our young from birth till they leave home, good or bad, right or wrong.

We are programmed about money based on how rich or poor our parents were and how they handled money. We were programmed about relationships, good or bad, based upon our parents' relationship. We were programmed regarding our eating habits, how we think, attitudes, and so on…good or bad.

Again all beliefs are false, until we decide they are true. The dictionary defines belief as, "to hold an opinion." We are programmed and convinced that our beliefs are true, whether they are true or not. In other words, we see and experience our beliefs as true. Two plus two equals four because we believe it does. If you believe that two plus two equals five, then no amount of argument will convince you otherwise, unless you choose to change that belief.

Beliefs equal truth because they are the mental sunglasses that filer your senses before you perceive the sensation. Your reticular activating system selects which sensory input is important based on your beliefs. Change a belief, and your view of the world changes, as well as the view others have of you.

Your beliefs color every bit of the input you receive. Only when you believe something do you become aware of the sensation of the input.

If our personal reality is based on core beliefs, then the universe that each of us experiences is not the cause but rather the effect of whatever is left over after our core beliefs do their work.

The statement, "I'll believe it when I see it" is backward. We actually see things *because* we believe them.

This has some amazing implications when you start to look at life in this way. Think about it. We see things *because* we believe it. Back to what I said earlier. When you change a belief, your view of the world changes.

So what is the answer to changing? The answer, or rather the challenge, is to take the negative past out of the present. The real goal should be to have your present empty of the negative past, and not to give your past meaning unless you say so.

Self-observation is the key.

Is what I'm giving energy right now taking me where I want to go? Is this fear or conflict supportive or non-supportive? Bottom line— is it true, or is it something you have been programmed to believe is true?

To change a belief, you have to challenge it.

Is it true?

What experience do you have that makes it true?

How do you know it to be true?

Who taught you to believe this?

What if they didn't know?

What if it's not true?

Who would you be without this belief?

What action should I take next?

When you achieve this level of control, you will experience what is known as true emotional freedom.

You'll have the freedom to choose fascination over frustration, success over failure, calm over upset.

When you take responsibility and observe reality… in other words what's really happening, you can then choose to create whatever reality you want.

Start today, by identifying a story you have been telling yourself that has been holding you back in life.

I can't get ahead financially. That's a story, not reality. It is not true unless you say it is.

I can't seem to keep a relationship together…

It's hard to lose weight…

Pick a story, just one to start. Look for the truth, then take action based upon that truth. The question is, does your interpretation of this story serve you or hold you back? Notice what you say to yourself about what has happened, and then exercise the freedom to choose a different interpretation.

I don't want you to believe me. I want you to try it and experience the result for yourself. You'll experience a positive result the very first time you try it.

Hey, and watch out for those predators!

***

To contact Jim:

www.JimBritt.com

www.PowerOfLettingGo.com

www.CrackingTheRichCode.com

www.FaceBook.com/JimBrittOnline

Jim Lutes

Having taught his branded form of human performance since the early 1990s, Mr. Lutes has accelerated top-level entrepreneurs throughout his career by conducting trainings on personal growth and subconscious programming into worldwide markets.

During this time, Jim took his skills regarding the human mind, and combining it with trainings on influence, persuasion, and communication strategies, he launched Lutes International in the early 1990s. Based in San Diego, California, Jim has taught seminars for corporations, sales forces, individuals, and athletes. Having appeared on television, radio, and worldwide stages, Jim's style, knowledge, and effectiveness provide profound results.

"Jim Lutes possesses a unique ability to create performance change in an individual in a fraction of the time it takes his competitors." The core of human decisions is based on the programs we acquire, reinforce, and grow. Combining Jim's various trainings, individuals can reach new levels of achievement and fulfillment in all areas of life. The results are at times nothing short of astonishing.

It's Not Where You Are, It's Where You're Going

By Jim Lutes

When we realize we yearn for change in our lives, at the beginning it can feel like we will be forever trapped in who we were or used to be. Indeed, the past is highly influential in our present life, whether we are aware of it or not. Past experiences inform all kinds of decisions we make in a day, some of which we make without thinking. When you decide to enter into a new relationship with someone, your past experiences may make you wary or afraid of being hurt. When you create a new piece of music or a piece of art, past experiences of how your creativity has been received will inform how you go about presenting that piece. When you really want to start to make change, first you have to allow yourself to be free of the past.

Consider: It's not where you are right now, but where you're going, and let this be among the primary motivators in getting you to take the necessary steps to change. This means looking forward, not looking back. Looking forward to who you want to be, not looking only at who you are right in this moment. It is a fine line to dance on, but being able to see the potential of who you are and how it can evolve as you decide to change your life is what will get you to a place of achieving your goals and desires.

Let me share with you two of the most motivating emotional states for creating change and success. These are inspiration and desperation. Desperation can be a good thing because until you get really dissatisfied, you won't do anything to take your life to another level. Dissatisfaction, then, is actually awesome! And dissatisfaction is an opportunity to turn struggle into something else. If you are feeling completely satisfied, you will become comfortable. When we feel comfortable, we are unlikely to make changes in our lives. Then life begins to deteriorate.

After all, it is not what you accomplish in relation to others that is important, it's what you accomplish in relationship to your own potential. Your tomorrow is based on your today, and once you realize that the ability to create your brightest tomorrow is already within you, you will start moving in the best direction for yourself, the direction of change for the better. You will move into an empowered place in the course of your own life.

Your brain is the most powerful computer on the planet. When you learn to use it properly, you can create any result you want. Your brain can give you the answer to almost any problem you have. The problem is that this computer we call our brain is not user-friendly, and does not come with an owner's manual. This book will show you how to operate your supercomputer with precision. Lasting change is not created in your life by learning more. Lasting change is created by dissolving the emotions, thoughts, patterns, beliefs, and programming that simply no longer serve you, in order to allow yourself to truly tap into your connection with Universal Power. You must re-design your blueprint to create the kind of results you want in your life.

This is the basis of the work I am inviting you to do with this book. Today, you are beginning a process that can truly change the quality of your life forever and can take that paint-by-numbers life you might be living now and create the masterpiece called your life. So just for a moment now, what I want you to do is imagine that your life is a painting. Imagine that you have died and are looking down at that painting. What did you leave behind? Is your life a masterpiece that is cherished and hangs prominently as an example for others of what is possible, or is it a paint-by-numbers life that is packed away in someone's basement?

Where you are in your life right now is the direct result of making decisions unconsciously, stuck in patterns and beliefs that served you once, but have not evolved to continue to serve you now, as an adult. If you feel stuck or are not pleased with your circumstances, being aware of the choices you make – choices that come from someplace other than your conscious thoughts - is step number one to taking control of your life. If you feel great about your life, you can also benefit from this work, as there are still doubtless limiting beliefs and thoughts in your subconscious mind that affect you too, whether you realize it or not.

It's not about where you are, it's about where you're going. If you want to change your life and align all major aspects of your life – finances, health, relationships, emotional wellbeing – then looking at what shaped you, and stepping out of a limiting identity, is what will help you to make the changes you seek. In other words, you must become the kind of person who holds and embodies the characteristics and qualities that you value. Visualizing it, affirming it, and even living your life by a new set of standards is not going to work long-term until this stuff goes from your conscious to your subconscious and finally into your heart. Not only do you have to DO it, and not only do you have to LIVE it, you also have to BECOME it. Then, you will manifest it.

For us to really live consciously, to be an example for others, then we have to be aware of what is shaping us. Be aware of what programs your subconscious mind is already running, be aware of how the conscious and subconscious mind work together, and be aware of the thoughts you think that are disempowering, and how you can change those thoughts to empowering ones.

It is always amazing to me how people take more time in a day to pick out what they are going to watch on television than on programming their minds. We spend more time choosing what kind of products we're going to use to clean our bodies than considering how we are going to clean our minds! We put so much emphasis on the external, when the reality is that the external is driven by the internal. If you want success in money, relationships, health and emotional health you must start to work from the inside out.

It all comes down to the power of your mind, and this includes both your conscious and subconscious mind. You have in your power the ability to transform your thoughts into your allies or your adversaries. You are creating your day through the thoughts you think. The subconscious mind is a direct connection to Universal Power, or source, or whatever higher power there is for you. The subconscious mind responds to images and emotions that come to your mind through your thoughts. You have in your life exactly what you tell yourself you want; that is, if you are frustrated, you're telling yourself you're frustrated. If you're saying "I'm sick," then you are not enjoying good health. Our internal communication is the dialogue we have with ourselves each day, and it is mostly filled with old programming. This is how our subconscious minds work, without our even being aware of how they are working behind the scenes to sabotage us. Our internal communication perpetuates the realization of what we expect.

If your internal communication is laden with limiting beliefs, or running on patterns that have been held in your subconscious for your whole life, then you will not be able to live to your fullest potential. Your patterns of thought and beliefs that no longer serve you must be sacrificed if you want to align all elements of your life. When I say "It's not where you are, it's where you're going", this is what I'm talking about. Where you are right now, as you read this, continues to be the self that is held hostage by an identity formed when you were a child. You are being held hostage by the patterns your subconscious mind is running in the background of your every waking moment. Until you reprogram your subconscious mind to make conscious choices in place of these choices made out of habit, you will not be able to move yourself out of where you might feel stuck and into where you will prosper. I'm not just talking about prosper financially either! I'm talking about prospering in whatever area you want to prosper – health, relationships, emotional wellbeing, sure, finances too. The big picture "prosper" - another word for it is thrive. To move from surviving to thriving means moving forward into where you're going, and not staying settled into where you are.

Take stock of where you are right now, and start to see where you can bridge the gap between where you are, and where you want to go. Where you are going in your life depends upon the choices you make today. Picking up this book was one choice you made that can serve you as you step forward more fully into your life. Eating a donut mindlessly on your drive home from work was one choice that may have been completely unconscious, one that may have served your eight-year-old self, starving for love from your mother, but one that doesn't serve your vision of being fit and strong. (Note that, occasionally indulging in a donut is ok, but making it a habit or doing it without thinking is not supporting your health goals.) By setting the intention to change, and deciding to make choices with awareness, through building smart connection between the subconscious and conscious minds, moment to moment, you will have a direct impact on each tomorrow as you build the future that you seek.

A close and careful read of this book is a unique opportunity to look deep inside yourself. Take a good look inside of your relationships, your decisions about money, and your decisions about your career, your relationship with the universe, or your higher power, and even your body. You will begin to understand how your own upbringing has influenced you and start identifying some of the decisions and habits you have created, including pinpointing one core decision that has affected your identity. Get clear about what really stands in your way (hint: it's you!)

Shifting your focus to become to become the kind of person you want to be has everything to do with YOU. If you want to change any circumstance or any relationship in your life, then you must begin with yourself no matter how convinced you are that something else or somebody else must change. This is where we begin to shift from blaming others for our circumstances and recognizing our own internal sense of agency and power in building and sustaining the life of our dreams. Recognizing the patterns and habits that keep you in a place of 'smallness' and fear is the first step. Then, as you begin to make shifts and changes, you will find yourself able to change even the most rigid system and stubborn person. I have experienced this myself. Every small change and shift is progress, and this moves you forward. Any movement forward, as a result of your desire and courage to make lasting changes creates the opportunity for every other part of your life to be moved forward as well. Everything is interrelated, especially the parts of our lives that comprise the whole of our lived existence.

The past may have a hold on your present, indeed, it is a tricky one to extricate yourself from, however you don't need to let it sit in the driver's seat. Taking control of your life and keeping a clear eye on the path ahead is one way of stepping out of the entanglement of the past. Use what you have learned, of course, but leave all that which is unnecessary. They call it 'baggage' for a reason! Where you are right now is the starting point for where you're going. It is okay, nay, even necessary, to imagine yourself as who you want to be, and to let these imaginings trump any more carryover of feelings associated with who you were. It's not where you are, or were, but where you're going that matters when you being on the journey of re-programming your subconscious mind.

***

To contact Jim:

Email: info@lutesinternational.com

Websites: www.lutesinternational.com

www.jimluteslive.com

Dr Spencer J. Holman

Dr. Spencer J. Holman is a Philosopher, innovative thought leader, CEO of multiple successful companies, and internationally recognized author and speaker. His work is an integral part of universities, judicial systems, schools, churches and many other social environments around the world.

He is the creator of the 10 Life Values Philosophy, a personal and relational success system which serves as a blueprint for men to be equipped with processes and tools for success multi-generationally and inter-generationally. He has helped over 1 million men improve their lives, their families and their communities. His best-selling books include: Fatherhood Legacy, Fatherhood Academy, The Spiritual Guide, The Wealth Management Guide, and The Black Person's Guide To Owning A Bentley.

Dr. Holman has 4 Doctoral degrees: honorary PhD in Philosophy, of which his 10 Life Values success system is based, honorary Doctorate in Naturopathy, of which his herbal formulations and training series are founded. His honorary Doctorate in Community Development is based on his work of enlightening over 1 million men in the United States and across 26 countries internationally. His earned PhD in Theology encompasses his one-on-one and peer counseling, the creation of his Spiritual Guide and work as a Minister and Chaplain.

The 10 Life Values: An Examined Life!

By Dr Spencer J. Holman

The ancient aphorism "Man know thyself" leads to many philosophers formulating arguments about the purpose and importance of knowing oneself. The Greek philosopher Pythagoras is often credited with saying "Man, know thyself, then thou shalt know the universe and God." Socrates is linked to the ancient dictum with this statement, "The unexamined life is not worth living." The ideology of knowing oneself leads to concern about the unexamined life but also presents the need for several questions. What standard should we use to examine our lives? What makes life worth living? Do we truly know what we value about life; what makes it worthwhile?

The work of historical philosophers continues into recent times with the dawn of the motivational speaker. Their application is rooted in self enlightenment and personal development and seeks to inspire people to examine their lives and evoke change through highly emotional experiences. Motivational speakers such as Dale Carnegie, Zig Ziglar, Jim Britt, Les Brown, and Tony Robbins are successful in getting us to see the need for personal development through the examination of our life. Other personal development leaders such as Stephen Covey with "The 7 Habits of Highly Effective People" and David Allen with his "Getting Things Done" methodology specialize in personal management systems. These systems complement the work of the philosophers as well as the motivational speakers.

Having studied and tested these ideologies, I would make the case that we should think carefully how we lead our lives. Do we know the value of life and do we know what we value about life? Building upon and expanding on the work of these great philosophers, motivational speakers and management system experts resulted in the creation of a conceptual framework for an emerging, comprehensive philosophy that I call "The 10 Life Values."

As I vigilantly stood on the shoulders of these giants for the past two decades, I collectively held in one hand the principles of self empowerment and personal development, and in the other hand the need for a powerful personal management system. The 10 Life Values is the culmination of a systemic, comprehensive success system that is woven into our every day life. It offers us the ability to fully understand and compartmentalize its findings for each dimension of our life, as well as the implications of those findings. It is a journey towards truth; leading to a full and satisfying life!

The 10 Life Values success system creates a new paradigm for personal examination, development, enrichment, and management that is easily incorporated into our modern lifestyle. This system is equipped with tools for examining, implementing, and recording each Life Value; not just as an essential pillar, but also as one in which the system is treated as a whole. The thrilling revelation is that the whole system is greater than the sum of its parts. Furthermore, it allows us to compartmentalize our life into meaningful categories so that we can collect all of the aspects of our life, manage them efficiently and achieve success in each area; thereby, achieving success in all areas. The 10 Life Values system represents an examined life!

Life Values are an inclusive collection, and interrelated system of the 10 most important areas of a person's life, regardless of cultural traditions and nuances. My initial work focused on men and fathers and is being expanded to address women, mothers and children. I conducted studies on over 5,000 male participants, investigating the theory that values are the central determining factor that propels a person towards success. The findings confirmed the fact that values are important; specifically, these 10 Life Values stand out within the hierarchy of values. It is clear that the role and importance of values was paramount in the decision making and behavior of each participant.

The outcomes of our study and fervent work with men over the past two decades have resulted in the well documented principle that a father whose life is examined from a value based perspective will contribute to his own success, the success of his family, and the indirect but much desired resulting success of the community and society. The reciprocal dynamic interrelated effect that individuals have on communities further signify the pivotal role value plays in every aspect of creating progressive people in communities around the world.

The 10 Life Values consist of Spiritual, Health, Family, Appearance, Dwelling, Mobility, Education, Profession, Leisure and Wealth. These values are grounded in love, faith, service, and excellence.

A simple definition of the 10 Life Values is:

> Spiritual Values: this value determines what we think and what we believe
>
> Health Values: this value reveals our physical, emotional and mental condition
>
> Family Values: this value shows who we are connected to and who we have relationships with
>
> Appearance Values: this value illustrates how we convey ourselves to the world
>
> Dwelling Values: this value declares where we live, grow and develop
>
> Mobility Values: this value explains the world around us and how we interact with it
>
> Education Values: this value affirms what we know; both our knowledge and intellect

Profession Values: this value acknowledges our contribution to the world

Leisure Values: this value proclaims how we choose to spend our personal time

Wealth Values: this value exposes both our accumulation of and possession of assets

Think of the 10 Life Values as your grandmother's delicious cherry pie. Imagine that the pie has 10 ingredients, each representing a Life Value that has its own intrinsic quality that complements and supports the other ingredients. Depending on your taste, some ingredients will stand out more than others and will have greater personal meaning and benefit. The Spiritual Value, one of the 10 ingredients and the bottom crust of the pie, is the foundation that holds the heavenly mixture together. The top layer has a cinnamon-butter crust covering the filling; this layer is the Wealth Value. Next, the fresh, hand-picked cherries are the main ingredient; the Health Value that works as a catalyst to optimize the flavor. Grandma's unique cherry pie recipe, the 10 Life Values, can be passed down creating and preserving generations of examined lives.

As I developed this philosophy, I noted other compelling features within the 10 Life Values. We express positive and negative values, overvalue and undervalue as well as devalue ourselves. When this happens, we need methods to prevent devaluation and ways to restore our values when they are compromised.

Positive values have a fundamental impact on successful living. These values are reflected in characteristics such as integrity, faith, peacefulness and trustworthiness. Positive values help us cope with difficulties and crisis. They offer us a framework to enhance peace, joy and love, providing an unshakable foundation for the very essence of life. We use positive values to fuel our drive for our innate need for love and power. Without a balance in our quest for love and power, we can overvalue, undervalue, and devalue ourselves. However, we can create, maintain and restore balance; thereby gaining freedom from constraints that hinder a fulfilled, examined life.

Negative values have a considerable fundamental impact on unsuccessful living. These values are reflected in behaviors such as anger, blame, corruption, and greed. Negative values can destroy our lives without our knowledge because these values are often deeply woven into the fabric of our being. Similar to positive values, we use negative values to fuel our drive for our innate need for love and power, but a life out of balance will result in overvaluation, undervaluation and devaluation of ourselves. The things that keep us from expressing healthy love and power, or push us into an exaggerated unhealthy display of love and power, can also hinder a fulfilled, examined life.

A deeper examination of the 10 Life Values reveals three factors that are necessary to collectively determine our value. The first factor defines how much we value ourselves; this is our self-worth. The second factor defines how much others value us and what we own; this is our currency. The final factor defines how much we value what others think of us; this is our personal net-worth. The relationship between these three factors; self worth, currency and net worth, is based on sound logic, proven philosophy and tested theory; and is incredibly plausible.

Our self-worth is connected to our values and is a major part of our identity. Identity refers to everything about us and our character. It defines who we are and shapes us by our set of closely held beliefs. The study of identity is approached differently among other disciplines; therefore, an interdisciplinary perspective is essential to bring the key tenets of identity into focus. Identity includes the concept of self, which influences our personality with characteristics that are unique to us. This unique personality coupled with how others view our personality type determines our view of ourself. Our sense of self hinges on our self-concept, which includes cognitive and affective processing systems.

Cognitive processing refers to how we think about and process ourselves. Affective processing refers to feelings, emotions and attitudes that get aroused and result in how we think and feel about ourself and others. Self-worth can be thought of cumulatively as confidence, competency and inferiority; again, shaped by our own self-concept and the internalized processing of how others perceive us, treat us and their expectations of us.

Currency is like water. It flows and moves dynamically and has the tendency to dissipate or overflow. Currency is a valuable medium of exchange and the concept of currency can be applied to all things of value. For instance, time has value, therefore, it is currency. Attention and knowledge also have value and thus are currency. At the center of the concept of currency is demand, which is a fluid social element because demand ebbs and flows depending on how valuable and available something is in life. The connection between demand and value is that the value of something is determined by the demand for it. This fact holds true for anything that we ascribe value to, and once demand is present we ascribe currency to it for exchange purposes.

When we think about how we use currency we discover that everyone has a value. For example, the homeless person on the street has several different currency levels based on the value placed on him by others. The person who gives money to the homeless person attributes currency (value) to him. The person who gives him a meal and sits down to listen to his story attributes a higher currency to him, and the person that steps right over him and wants him to die, attributes no value to him at all.

How much do we value what others around us think of us? How much we value the thinking and opinion of others as a measurement of ourselves is considered our personal net-worth. This third factor is an important principle because it can be a hinderance to people that place tremendous value in what others think of them. Without seeing what others think of them as merely one of three dimensions that contribute to value, self-concept and identity, the ones that place too much value in what others think can become debilitated and wind up being perpetual people pleasers. This flaw doesn't have to be a life sentence, it can be changed.

Properly and consistently applying these concepts to our life requires having a robust system with tools that can adapt to the changing needs of our life. The requisite system is one that can not only meet us where we are and address our immediate needs, but also can conform to our growth patterns and changes in our life and lifestyle. The 10 Life Values can serve to mend what is broken in our life or enhance our current level of function if we are already doing well. It's a system for management and organization after an evaluation and assessment have been completed. The power of this system is in its simple yet complex proven results. The system is sequential and ordered, yet not rigid. It is precise yet also customizable. It is a system that can be implemented in everyday life, creating synergy and producing overall success in our life.

It's important to look at our life at this moment in time, not what used to be or what we used to have. We should not look at our identity as defined by a title from the past, but who are we right now. If we start from where we are currently, the 10 Life Values can work on our current reality and get us to our desired reality. It will become a new, examined way of life.

The 10 Life Values success system is designed to either be self-directed, taught in a classroom by a facilitator or implemented with a coach. Ultimately, the resulting effect is the development of a skill-set that will identify our internal guide and help us to follow it. Following the system is an important step in sustainable growth because our internal guide stays within us and gets activated when we encounter both positive and negative triggers in life. This internal guide governs our perspectives, decisions, priorities, and interactions with others and with the world. It serves as a compass for what we chose to do and how we spend our time, money and resources.

The 10 Life Values success system teaches us how to use these tools to become highly organized to expedite the process of utilizing time management fundamentals. The system incorporates the important dimensions of planning, organizing and managing as well as a hierarchical system to help us examine, implement and measure our success on a daily basis.

Our new daily habit of using the 10 Life Values can be implemented using a traditional filing cabinet, a mobile folder system, note taking and management software such as Evernote, Google Keep, Simplenote, Microsoft OneNote, or remote cloud storage systems such as DropBox Paper. Other ways our system is seamlessly integrated is on iOS and Android devices using folders for the corresponding app as well as desktop and laptop computers using file management systems, calendar, reminders, and email inboxes. These applications are extremely useful tools that track each component of the 10 Life Values. Many of us use the 10 Life Values system to support our parenting, leadership, mentorship and community service as well as gives us a system to evaluate our progress as mothers, fathers, coaches, mentors and caregivers.

While there is a lot of research, theorizing and conversation going on about values, the 10 Life Values are positioned uniquely to create lasting individual, family, community and global impact. This system consistently and strategically offers methods and tools for evaluation, examination, management, organization and hierarchical ordering of essential components of our lives. This system will enhance personal enrichment and personal management in order to produce a fulfilled, examined life.

The prevailing questions remain: What do you value? How do you determine what you value? What is the value of every aspect of your life based on? Is your valuation haphazard or ordered? Does what you value serve you to get you from your current reality to your desired reality? Does what you value help bring you into a deeper alignment with God and His plan for your life? Does what you value help you to accurately determine your net-worth? If you were challenged by answering any of these questions you are not alone. But know that there is a better way. Know that The Change has been revealed for you. Accept it through the power of each stellar and enduring pillar of the 10 Life Values.

I want to thank the one million men who have been exposed to the 10 Life Values through the Father's Time Fatherhood Academy and the thousands of men, fathers, grandfathers, mentors and everyone that has been gracious enough to sit in my classrooms since 2008 discovering their 10 Life Values. Furthermore, I want to thank you for embarking on this journey with me. If you know of anyone who needs help discovering where they've been, where they are and where they need to go, please introduce them to the 10 Life Values system. I would be honored to share these inspired gifts which I have formulated for individual peak performance. We are on a mission to change the world, one examined life at a time!

***

More about the author

Dr. Spencer J. Holman founded and incorporated his company, Father's Time, in 1998. This allowed him to manifest his vision of the 10 Life Values Philosophy, which he developed at the youthful age of 18. His mission was clear: motivate men to strive for excellence in every fundamental domain of life, from spiritual growth to wealth creation and management.

Prior to founding Father's Time, Dr Holman's career began in the United States Marine Corps where he honorably served our country and was presented with several prestigious awards, medals and certificates throughout his career. After retiring from the Marine Corps, Dr. Holman entered another successful career in Mortgage Banking and seized the opportunity to create strategic ways to increase wealth and economic growth in low income and emerging markets. Today after two decades of successfully serving men with the 10 Life Values, these principles are being expanded to serve women and youth. Dr. Holman is currently the Assistant Dean of Online Learning for a rapidly growing seminary and university that has adopted the 10 Life Values Philosophy and where his Fatherhood Academy Curriculum is offered. He is the creator of their innovative, state of the art, comprehensive online platform, and the visionary behind their strategy for global impact through certificate and accredited programs, courses and degrees to make learning accessible for all.

***

To Contact Dr. Holman:

phone: +1-951-515-5117

email: staff@fatherstime.com

website: www.fatherstime.com

LinkedIn: spencer-holman

Facebook: spencer.holman.77

Skype: spence767

YouTube: FathersTime

Christine Suva

Christine Suva has spent a lifetime exploring her insatiable passion for personal and professional development! She's a Certified Professional Life & Career Coach, Executive Coach, Speaker, Consultant, two-time Amazon #1 International Best Selling Author and interviewed for television and radio. As Founder and President of THRIVE Coach Services, Inc., she is deeply committed to helping others find passion, purpose and success in their lives! Her business is the culmination of over 20 years' experience guiding thousands across the country to achieve career and personal goals as an Outplacement Consultant and Wellness Professional in the education, healthcare, corporate, and community settings.

Chris specializes in: success mindset strategies, executive branding, communication, storytelling, transition and reinvention. Her approach is holistic bringing together her wellness, counseling, coaching and career development/transition experience. Her clients are often seeking more meaning and purpose in their lives and improved ability to inspire, engage and lead others. Chris feels deep gratitude for being called to her highest purpose in her work and enjoys helping others discover, develop and live out their highest calling in their lives.

Mastering Your Mindset for Success!

By Christine Suva

"Marilyn!" "Yes, Mom?" "Come in here, please." At 22, tall, slim, with light brown hair; Marilyn Spencer was beautiful and full of youthful energy. She bounded into the dining room. "What is it?" she asked, noticing her mom was clearly excited. "There's a concert at Kiel Auditorium in 3 weeks. The pianist had to back out, and they want you to take his place!" Her mom whispered excitedly holding the phone to her chest. "It's Gershwin's 'Rhapsody in Blue', and you'd be playing with an orchestra. I think you should do it. Can you learn it and have it memorized in time?" "Yes, I believe I can!" "She'll do it!" Marilyn prayed that God would help her do what seemed impossible.

It was 1957. Kiel Auditorium was the largest arena in St. Louis seating 9,300. She practiced tirelessly. Three weeks later, in her beautiful floor length gown, she gave a perfect performance! Her hard work, belief in her abilities and strong faith allowed her to take big risks, and each time her talent and confidence grew.

For context, it's important to learn a little about Marilyn's personal life. She and her brother, Don lived in a 4 flat apartment building their parents owned across from the Missouri Botanical Garden along with grandparents, aunts and uncles. She had a rich family life, spending many evenings with family and friends playing in the garden until bedtime. They helped her feel grounded and connected to something larger than herself. For Marilyn, family came first. Period! By learning to pursue her passion balanced with her values and priorities; she learned to make the best choices for herself. She knew what she was willing to sacrifice and what was non-negotiable, and learned to trust her instincts. The foundation for building a life without regrets was being set.

At eight years old, she began piano lessons with her mother, a graduate of the Conservatory of Music and an accomplished pianist herself. She worked hard to develop her gift with thousands of hours of practice, concerts, and recitals on the radio in St. Louis. At thirteen, she'd been offered a scholarship to Juilliard, the world-renowned performing arts school. It was an opportunity of a lifetime! She asked herself, "Is traveling the world as a concert pianist MY dream? Am I willing to uproot my family or go alone across country to pursue that dream?" "No." Marilyn felt a profound sense of purpose sharing her gift, but knew she must find a way to share it while honoring her highest value of family to be truly happy.

She studied Music Education at Washington University and, over a 35 year career, instilled the love of music in thousands of children! She took time off when her kids were young, and was the choir director and organist at church. She played for special events at Medinah Temple and Orchestra Hall, Chicago and was the accompanist for the professional show "A Chorus Line". In retirement, she'd still sit at her grand piano and practice for hours. Why? Because she loved it! It's what she was MADE for!

Now I have a question for you. Did she pursue her life's purpose even though she said "No" to Juilliard? Absolutely! She joyfully created her legacy while staying in alignment with her values and priorities. Reinventing herself to honor her stage in life, she expressed her passion in multiple ways, in multiple environments, at multiple levels. Marilyn never lost sight of her highest priority of family and made decisions with that in mind. She knew that traveling the world as a concert pianist would not give her the family life she wanted most. Her involvement in music was lifelong and she never stopped learning and growing. THAT is how you create a life without regrets and leave your legacy to the world! And THAT is what I want most for YOU!

How to Think Bigger about WHO you are, WHAT you do and WHY

After spending over 20 years as a wellness professional, outplacement consultant and now in my Life & Career Coaching business; I've helped thousands of individuals and groups interested in personal and professional development. Their goals have included improving their wellness, becoming more effective leaders or reinventing their life and career to find more meaning and fulfillment. In many cases, they appeared to have it all, but felt empty and often guilty for wondering, "Is this all there is?" They needed a change. Some knew what they wanted but weren't making progress. Others had no idea what they wanted or where to start.

There's nothing I love more than helping people discover their calling, building their confidence to OWN it, and equipping them to share it! It's not easy. Most things worth having aren't. Achieving success does take sacrifice and change, but you need to know what your non-negotiables are; to know yourself well enough to let YOUR sense of purpose, values and priorities guide you.

Why Am I Here?

If you've ever felt you've lost your identity and felt you were barely hanging on, consider this: You are NOT your job! You are NOT your title, company or business! You are NOT your bank account, car or house! You are far bigger than any roles you play or any material thing you'll ever own! You are here to do what only you can do in your unique way. What were you born to do? If you're not clear, that's ok. It's an unfolding process and worth the work to uncover it. You simply cannot build a life you love without knowing who you are.

I know from personal experience that reinvention is a process of coming back to yourself. In 1995, my life turned upside down in 5 days. Monday, I broke off a serious relationship. Tuesday, I found out my job had been eliminated in a merger. Wednesday, I planned to sign a new lease and move in Friday. Instead, I moved 1 ½ hours away, back in with my parents at 28, in a new community. My sister,

Jenny said, "God has something entirely different planned for you!" It was the darkest time in my life. Even though some of those changes were good and my choice, having all of them happening at once was overwhelming! I had to turn every tool I had as a wellness professional on myself to completely reinvent my life. Things transformed when I realized I had the opportunity to consciously choose what I wanted to create. My life was a fresh canvas, and I had the paintbrush!

That job, encompassed much of my purpose, yet had become frustrating and no longer fit. I wasn't a quitter and thought, "It'll get better," but I felt burnt out and my passion was fading. Sometimes, when we don't listen to that inner voice saying, "It's time for a change," God and the universe will make that change FOR us – a job loss, the end of a relationship, etc. I received outplacement and secured the perfect job for me. Two years later, I married my wonderful husband, Tom!

Life has taught me that beautiful beginnings often follow our darkest times. During that difficult time, my faith, family and friends helped keep my hope alive. I trust the process of reinvention and am grateful that my world fell apart back then. I wouldn't be where I am today if it hadn't! I realized that I'm stronger and more resilient than I ever imagined! The value of every lesson, tool, and strategy it took for me to find my way out is forever etched in my heart.

When defining your purpose, it should:

- Come naturally to you
- Engage your gifts and strengths
- Be something you love so much you'd do it for free (and probably have)
- Allow for lifelong involvement

Common mistakes when defining your purpose:

- Defining it too narrowly by a specific job title, company, business or role
- Inability to express it in multiple ways at multiple levels
- Letting others decide what you should do and who you should be
- Inability to reinvent with life stages and shifting priorities

What's Your Golden Thread?

Look back over your life to discover your "Golden Thread", those elements that have tied together your experiences and sense of self. Typically, there's overlap between your education, training, interests and jobs you've held. What's consistent? The table below is an example from my background.

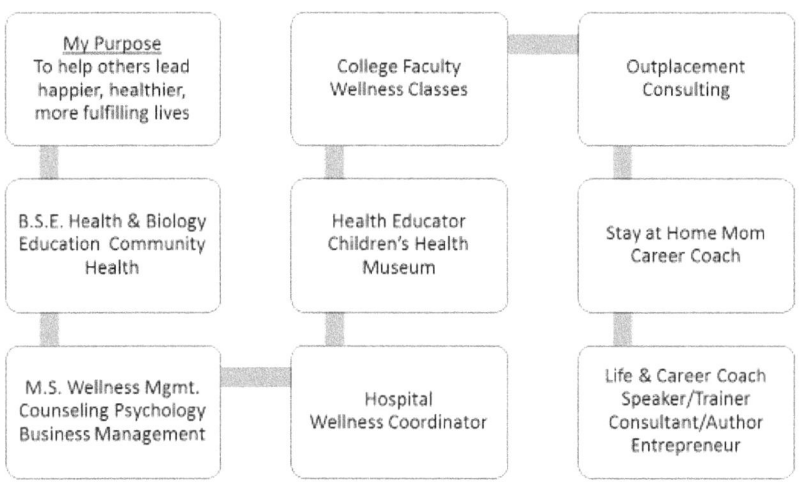

I discovered my purpose in my teens which guided everything I've done since! It's like an internal compass that keeps me on track. Try this for yourself. Look for the overlap of roles, skills and interests. This helps you begin learning to tell your story. You may be surprised by what it reveals! By sharing our stories, we communicate what makes us unique and share our message.

Begin by asking:

- When have I felt totally on fire? What was I doing, and with whom?
- What am I most passionate about?
- What can I do and completely lose track of time?

Living a life of meaning and purpose is not "all or nothing", nor is it a "one and done" thing. Staying involved with your passion can mean everything from watching concerts on television to traveling the world as a musician and everything in between. When you define your purpose that way, you can reinvent it lifelong. Think back to Marilyn from the beginning. Most people assume we should all want the "pinnacle" position in our field. Yet, if Marilyn had pursued traveling the world as a concert pianist, she would have denied herself the family life she wanted most. So, she found a way to do both that worked for her.

What if you aren't clear on your purpose? What if others focused more on what you're not than WHO you are growing up? In some families, acknowledging your talents is frowned upon. This can make it difficult to know your purpose or find direction and creates limiting beliefs that get in the way. A mentor or coach can help!

Resistance, self-doubt and old programming will rise up when you're pushing your self-imposed boundaries. If you expect it as a normal part of the process, you can avoid letting fear take hold and derail your movement forward.

Master Your Mindset

The most pervasive hindrance to creating a fulfilling, successful life is your mindset. Many who are outwardly successful feel empty on the inside and trapped by the "golden handcuffs" of a good salary, benefits, and title. They desperately want a change, but don't know where to start. A variety of blocks come up:

"What will my spouse, family, friends, colleagues think?"

"It's not logical. Why would I leave security and success for an unknown?"

"I have a family to care for. It's too risky."

"It's all about the kids now. What I want doesn't matter anymore."

"What if I fail?"

"What if I succeed, and my life changes too much?"

"Making my passion my job will ruin it."

"It's too late to change."

It breaks my heart. We were not created to be miserable! I believe in being responsible and don't recommend making big changes haphazardly. However, I've also seen what being "responsible" does when that means working in a spirit crushing job that poisons a person's life. Many pay for it with broken relationships, a devastating health crisis, addictions and even death. NO JOB is worth that! It's possible to build a life of happiness and fulfillment and still be responsible.

Mastering your mindset involves learning to master your energy. Science has proven that everything alive is made of and emanates energy. A good analogy is to think of your energy as a radio frequency. There are multiple energetic frequencies like tuning a radio and the energy you transmit either works for or against you. By learning to shift your energy, you can attract people, circumstances and situations you want with less stress and more success. People who resonate at a low frequency are those with "victim thinking", often complaining that everyone else has it easier. This kind of thinking literally repels success. We see that in the workplace. Negative corporate cultures flood corporate America. Many of my clients are highly valuable employees who are tired of working in a toxic environment and want me to help them get out! Part of the problem is the prevalence of "conflict energy". When the organizational culture is one of competition and mistrust, where employees horde information as power rather than working together and leaders lead by intimidation, everyone suffers, including the company bottom line.

I work with executives on branding, communication, storytelling and transition. Those in transition often think their resume is what keeps them from securing a new position. Typically, it's not their resume, but their mindset that's in the way. They're used to thinking logically and tactically so naturally go to something concrete like their resume often tweaking it endlessly. Their resume can be impeccable, but if their mindset disempowers them, that resume won't matter! Many have had great success and are used to being someone others come to for help. It can be difficult to admit they're struggling with self-doubt and fear. With their confidence rattled, they may lose sight of their abilities and accomplishments and find it difficult to tell their own story. As a result, they begin behaving in counterproductive ways. They hide behind the computer, and don't network or follow up. When they don't hear back or get a negative response, it only fuels their belief that they may never regain ground professionally. This can become a self-fulfilling prophecy. By helping them release their fear by grounding them in their value, we unpack and repack their story to build their executive brand and shift their mindset so they can get into effective action. With their confidence and clarity restored, they can present their story and what they're looking for with ease and success!

Many new coaches and speakers doubt their value or lack clarity on their message and hold back. They tweak their website and blog posts, spend hours on trainings because, "It's not perfect yet." Meanwhile, those they're meant to serve suffer waiting to find them. Success requires constant expansion of their mindset. Sadly, many quit just before they would have had the transformation they've been seeking.

Build A Vision

When you aren't sure where you want to go, you can stay stuck - sometimes for decades. When you have a powerful, clear, compelling vision, and you've learned to shift your energy; it can pull you into action toward success! "Pain pushes until vision pulls!"

If you don't have YOUR vision, begin by asking:

- Why am I here?
- What are my strengths, skills, passions, values and priorities?
- What do I want my life to look like at this stage?
- What legacy do I want to create and why?

To get something different, you've got to be willing to DO something different! Build a vision for the legacy you want to create and take action in that direction.

In Closing:

Marilyn is my mom! Her choice to stay in St. Louis and study music education led to her daily practice in an auditorium at Washington University, where a handsome young man would quietly slip in to hear her play. Weeks later, he finally got the nerve to stay and introduce himself.

John Gillham was also very accomplished from a young age. He was class president and a district leader in the United Methodist Youth Program. They fell in love. Just prior to proposing, he was approached regarding a Rhodes Scholarship to Oxford University – considered the most prestigious scholarship in the world! He too was faced with a critical decision and chose to marry the woman he loved over the very impressive invitation to study abroad. They moved to Yale University where John graduated from seminary. He pastored churches for more than 40 years, counseling, teaching adult classes and mentoring seminary students. In retirement, they continued to spend summer evenings on Chicago's lakefront at Millennium Park listening to the orchestra play beautiful music under the stars.

I share their story because they have exemplified what living a life of meaning and purpose in alignment with your values and priorities looks like. They modeled intentional decision making; even if, to the outside world, those choices didn't fit with what they "should" want. It's because of my parents that I do this work! Their example of choosing to live life without regrets is one of their greatest gifts to me. Their consistent drawing my attention to my own gifts and encouragement to develop and share them has allowed me to live my life the same way. Those lessons were invaluable and are what I now share with others.

My clients are intelligent, motivated, success minded people who get offered incredible opportunities. Yet, not every opportunity is right for everyone. It takes an awareness of what gives your life meaning, grounding yourself in your values, and a willingness to prioritize personal alignment to make better decisions. This intimate understanding of who you are is the foundation for successfully moving forward. Otherwise, you can find yourself filled with regret in a life you don't want.

Over the last 3 years, my mom developed Alzheimer's and suffered multiple strokes until her passing. Losing her was devastating. Yet, I had the profound realization that she was still teaching me! She was revealing the POWER of having lived her life that way - sharing the gift she was MADE to share in alignment with her values, leaving nothing unsaid and nothing undone. The comfort and peace it brought for her and our family was priceless! She played life full out. You can't ask for more than that! Now, it's my calling - my mission - to help others embrace their gifts, confidently OWN them, and enable them to THRIVE!

***

To contact Christine:

Founder & President of THRIVE Coach Services, Inc. – 630-427-7432

www.thrivecoachservices.com

www.linkedin.com/in/christinesuva

Craig Wayne Boyd

Rooted in the southern tradition of country music and topped with a rebellious flair, Craig is an extreme talent who excelled at singing and playing the guitar at age of four. He received long-due critical and mainstream recognition as the Season 7 winner of The Voice. Taking the title as a member of Team Blake (Shelton), Craig dazzled the audience with the premiere performance of "My Baby's Got A Smile on Her Face," which debuted #1 on the Hot Country Songs chart, becoming the second song (following Garth Brooks' "More Than A Memory") to ever do so.

Growing up in the Dallas, Texas suburb of Mesquite, Craig's childhood was highly influenced by gospel and country music and he later became the choir director at his hometown church. After a trip to Nashville, life-changing events came his way. Craig signed a publishing deal with EMI and after several years of prolific songwriting, he began touring heavily, logging more than 1,000 shows in four years, and opening for acts like Jamey Johnson, Randy Houser and Brantley Gilbert. In 2015, Craig opened up for Rascal Flatts during their *Vegas Riot!* nine-show residency at the Hard Rock Casino in Las Vegas before continuing on his headlining *West Bound and Down Tour*.

I'm Still Here

By Craig Wayne Boyd

"Life is made up of all these tidbits. What you do with them, and how you use them, is what dictates the rest of your life, so concentrate on the small things" ~ Bob Spear

A wise man named Bob Spear once told me, "Life is made up of all these tidbits; what you do with them and how you use them, is what dictates the rest of your life, so concentrate on the small thing". For me, those tidbits always had something to do with music. It's always been a part of me. I grew up surrounded by music… whether I was singing in my church choir, school plays, listening to music or completely devoting myself to learning the instruments I picked up at garage sales. I knew music was in my future because I couldn't get enough of it. Which musical path to take was something I struggled with early in my life. As the son of a honky-tonk player and a mother who raised me to sing gospel. I was constantly conflicted until the pastor of my church, explained to me that you can't always preach to the choir and to go where I was led.

I wasn't sure what all of that meant until I was 23. My father and I travelled to Nashville where I was fortunate enough to meet a very prominent person in the music publishing scene and play a few songs for him that I'd written in Dallas. He told me I was on the right track but that I had to be present to win and then he asked if I was willing to move to Music City and start a new journey. I never thought twice about it. I said *"Yes"* surprising myself with no hesitation. On the way home I looked up and said, *"God, is this what I'm really supposed to do?"*

We can sometimes question ourselves out of our dreams, not realizing it. After all, I'd just built a new house, I was married & I had a stable six figure job... was I going to do this and did it even make sense? The answer came to me like a 2x4 across the forehead when I pulled up to my house and found a note from my then wife. She had left me along with specific instructions not to try to find her.

Shortly thereafter I became extremely depressed. I lost my sales job and one rainy night in Texas, I rolled and totaled my truck. Being told I was lucky to be alive, I wasn't feeling very *lucky* but I knew that God had given me my answer. Six months later, I was on my way to Nashville with everything I could pack in the back of an old farm truck my father had loaned me.

After moving to Nashville, it seemed as if I was on my way to fulfilling my dream. I was writing with some great songwriters, performing in writers' rounds, and formed the trio, Southland, with musicians Cole Lee and Levi Sims. A year later I landed a publishing deal with EMI, one of the most renowned publishing companies in the world. For 3 years, life was good. The trio was getting positive attention, we had labels interested in us, and we were playing packed venues. You know if there's one thing the music industry will teach you, over and over again... don't hold your breath. Before I knew it, my trio had broken up, I had lost my publishing deal, and close friend and former band mate, Levi, had passed away from cystic fibrosis. I was back to square one, grieving the loss of my friend, and trying to figure out how to pick up the pieces. Bob's words would swim through my head, "tidbits, and what you do with them, concentrate on the small things". I hung on to these words.

After much contemplation I decided to pursue a solo career. I took the heartache of the last few years into the studio and recorded an album to reflect the highs and lows of my life. I found new band members and hit the road... playing gigs from Minot, North Dakota to Key West, Florida and everywhere in between. I was introduced to a new independent label in Nashville and we recorded another album to reflect the *determination* that I had to finish what I started. The single from that album was a direct reflection of my journey so far; aptly titled, ***"I Ain't No Quitter"***. We even made a video and submitted the single to radio where it began climbing the charts. Finally, I was back! The single reached the top 30's on the Music Row Charts, defying the precedent at the time that if you weren't on a major label it was nearly impossible to get a song played. I was determined to break the Nashville mold and be an independent artist with a hit single. I'd been playing nearly 250 dates a year, including a radio tour where I visited every radio station that would have me. And don't hold your breath again! When I returned from one of my radio tours, I saw movers pulling furniture out of my independent label's office. My immediate thought was, "Awesome! We're getting new furniture", but the reality was that the company had lost its funding. Even with my single still moving up the charts, I was headed back to square one once again.

No label, no money to pay band members, no gigs and back to the drawing board. It was 2012, strike three.

I'm not sure if it was my "stupidity" or "stick-to-itiveness" that kept me going, but I know most sane people would have packed it in and given up. By now, I was a new father to my first child, a son Jaxon, who had become a new inspiration in my life. It wasn't just about me anymore and I had the pressing responsibility to be successful and do what I knew to do to support him. My current single, *"I Ain't No Quitter"*, was supposed to define me and yet there I was, standing at a crossroads, trying to decide if I had the strength to move forward. The answer was yes, because ***I was not a quitter and I would find a way figure it out***. I started over again and for 2 years I played as many gigs that I could on the road, supplementing income wherever I could to support my son. I picked up jobs working construction while also writing and performing as often as possible. I will never forget this one day in particular, I was working on a job site when a Nashville label executive came into the house we were building and recognized me. He looked at me and asked, "Aren't you Craig Wayne Boyd, what are you doing here?" I told him I had a son to support now and needed to pick up some extra work. I've never been ashamed of who I am, and don't get me wrong, hard work has never beneath me, but in this moment I truly felt defeated. This isn't where I wanted to be, it was where I had to be.

I began questioning God's plan for me… was music really the route I was intended to pursue? Had I already used up all of my chances or was there another lesson, another road I had travel to find my way?

My landlord had just given me 30 days to move out and it seemed like I was being pushed in another direction. Nearly homeless and out on the road, I'd just had a heart to heart with my drummer about quitting music and concentrating on another career. I didn't want to give it up, but I needed something stable so I could confidently support my son. With quitting on my mind I opened up my computer, only to find an email from a producer of the NBC TV show The Voice, asking if I would be interested in auditioning for season 7 of the series. I thought it was spam. Turns out, it wasn't. After debating whether or not I wanted to be in a televised singing competition, I felt this opportunity must have been put in my path for a reason. The challenge was mentally preparing to head to L.A. With no official place to call home, I spent the weeks leading up to my audition packing up my things, moving them into storage and sleeping on any sofa available, in hopes that something would come of this next venture. *This is when I decided if this didn't work, I would have to give in to quitting, which I dreaded.*

"To me it was never a competition against other contestants, it was more of a competition against me and my own inner demons telling me I couldn't do this"

When I arrived in L.A, I began questioning everything about myself. Was this how I wanted to further my career? Was I cheating the system? But with much soul searching, I decided that finding the best way to achieve your goals is not cheating, it's changing your way of doing things and thinking outside of the box. If this was the opportunity that was being laid out before me, then I was going to do my best, no matter what the outcome. During one of the many vetting interviews, ***I was told by one of the producers that I was "positive to a fault".*** That was funny to me because little did they know the internal battle going on inside me. No matter what, I couldn't let anyone else know how distraught I was because I knew positive affirmation was the only way I was going to move ahead.

With my mind focused on doing *"my very best"*, I flew through the audition process, landed on Blake Shelton's team and was paired up for my first battle. I knew this was a contest against other people on the show with the object being to beat the other artists... but to me it was never a competition against the others. It was more of a fight with myself and my own inner demons telling me I couldn't do this. When the first battle was over, I stood in front of my coach and was not chosen to move on. Rejection is not fun for anyone, especially when it's nationally televised, but I looked inward and knew I'd done my best. As I was about to walk off the stage, knowing if this was the end of the road for me, then I could accept it and move on to that next chapter of my life, the lights flashed, buzzers went off and I was saved by Gwen Stefani, another coach on The Voice. Relief flowed through me as I realized I'd been given another chance to prove I belonged there.

They say, "If you wanna hear God laugh, tell him your plan"! Apparently going home was NOT on HIS agenda. The following week, I was put up against another artist on Team Gwen. I was once again defeated in the 2nd battle and about to step off the stage when the lights went off, the buzzer sounded and Blake Shelton was stealing me back to his team! I can't explain the rush of emotion I felt in those 30 seconds between being rejected by Gwen and then saved again by Blake, but if I had to try, it would be like falling off a cliff and right before you hit the dirt, something swoops in and catches you. You don't know if you're crying because you're still reeling from the fear of falling or the relief of being saved.

Reflecting back, connecting the dots, it was the same thing that had been going on in my life prior to the show. Only this time it was on television in front of millions of people, in a shorter amount of time, but with the same outcomes. I was denied, then saved, denied and saved again. The challenge ahead would not just be to prove myself to my coach, but to the voting public.... Little did I know that I already had.

As the show went "Live" and the viewers were able to decide my fate, I pushed on as I always did. Keeping faith in myself that I was doing the right thing from week to week. The struggle wasn't in the choice of songs or how I would perform them, that part was easy because I'd been doing that for 10 years prior. It was in the seconds before my name was called to stay, wondering if America understood me or if they would decide I fell short of their expectations. The fans never disappointed, they never wavered. So, as true as they were to me, I stayed true to myself. Time after time I challenged myself, never to focus on the other contestants song choices or if I could beat them. I made many friends, offered advice to whomever asked and helped them out in their performances. I knew the outcome would be whatever was meant to be.

The weeks flew by and I found myself at the moment of truth. It was down to the final Top 4. As I was walking though set, someone yelled "Hey! There's Craig Wayne Boyd!" and without thinking, I responded *"Yep! I'm Still Here"!*

In that moment it hit me. All my life I lived in that moment of the song, "I Ain't No Quitter" I'd released to radio all those years back and now I was living its sequel. Never giving up, never giving in to those demons that constantly nagged at my subconscious telling me I couldn't do it and I knew I needed to write that song. I took pen to paper and began writing.

The Change[16]

Those who know my story and those that watched Season 7 of NBC's The Voice know the outcome but to touch briefly on that moment; I remember being on the stage with the last 4 contestants. I was the only member left from Team Blake and the other 3 were from Team Adam. We huddled together on the stage in front of a live audience as the results slowly dwindled our numbers from four to two. I watched Damien walk off first, then Chris, wondering how it was possible that I would be left to stand alone with Matt. Once again would my hopes be dashed? I'd never set out to win the show, I had come here to prove to myself that I could stand with the best and that I was worthy of being here. There I was, in the final moments, suddenly I wanted it so badly. Although I could accept second place…would this be the moment I was triumphant? Or would it turn out like every other time, where I reached up, and could feel my dreams within my grasp only to have them slip through my fingers? Would I have to "tuck my tail" and run back to Nashville to start all over? Would I have to take another career path to support my son? Where would I live? If things had gone differently, my guess is that because of my determination, I would have found a way to stay with music in some form or fashion. That's the way I was taught. It was bred in me to be that "nose to the grindstone" type of guy, and I knew I still had more fight in me.

Call it luck, call it fate, call it divine intervention, but as it turned out, I didn't have to worry about any of those questions. My name was called and I was crowned the winner of season 7 of The Voice. In that moment of realization, I thought back to Bob Spears and his wise words for me when I was 17:

Each point in my life when my dreams were shattered, I pulled some knowledge from his statement as I would pick myself back up and moved forward. Each challenge, each disappointment, each victory was a tidbit I kept with me and learned from to make the next moment better. I never realized how powerful his words were until then. I knew as I held the trophy in my hand, confetti falling around me and tears in my eyes, I had conquered a mountain by simply believing in myself... and so begins a grand new journey and next chapter of my life. What will it hold?

I'm Still Here
Written By:
Craig Wayne Boyd, Arlis Albritton & Josh Helms

I'm a believer, but there's a song in me that's begging to be heard

Yes, I'm a dreamer, hanging on to hope for everything its worth

So I skipped a few meals and slept in my car

When you're down that low they don't care who you are

In this who-do-ya-know town

Oh but look at me now

I'm still here

Standing strong

Giving it my all

Cause that's just who I am

I won't give up

I don't know what that means

It's not inside of me

To pack my bags and turn my back

Walk away just like that and disappear

I'm still here

I'm no leaver, but I gotta be where the marquee holds my name

The Change[16]

Because I'm a singer, so I move town to town and stage to stage

But my sons at home and he's too young to know, why sometimes daddies have to go

So I point to his heart and say, son, if you ever need me, right here's where I'll be

I'm still here

Standing strong

Giving it my all

Cause that's just who I am

I won't give up

I don't know what that means

It's not inside of me

To pack my bags and turn my back

Walk away just like that and disappear

I'm still here

No, I won't give up

I don't know what that means

It's not inside of me

To pack my bags and turn my back

Walk away just like that and disappear

I'm still here

I'm still here

I'm still here

***

To contact Craig:

Website: http://www.craigwayneboyd.com

Facebook: htttps://www.facebook.com/Craigwayneboyd

Twitter: https://www.twitter.com/cwbyall

Instagram: https://www.instagram.com/cwbyall

Snapchat: Cwbyall

YouTube: https://www.youtube.com/Craigwayneboyd

Bill Holmes

Bill Holmes is a marketing creative director and communications strategist with a broad range of experience and achievement – training ... meetings ... events – all are within his purview.

Early in his career, Bill spent several years at Fieldcrest Cannon as National Account Manager. He was instrumental in the development of the first fully licensed Martha Stewart Program within K-Mart, for which he was twice awarded the Edward Cosper Industry Award for Marketing Excellence.

He's held several positions in the pharmaceutical industry, where he developed co-marketing campaigns for several leading food, drug and mass merchant retailers.

Since then, Bill has partnered on meetings, events and other communications projects in the healthcare and pharmaceutical industries. He's worked within many therapeutic classes and created unique branding and marketing communication initiatives for Pfizer, Novartis, Bristol-Myers Squibb, IBM, Merck, Abbott, Lilly, GlaxoSmithKline and Philips Electronics.

Bill also has extensive experience and background in Instructional Design and Learning & Performance Improvement. He has served as the CEO of Montage Connective Marketing focusing on Business Improvement Process, Life Coaching. He's also authored several presentations focusing on Behavior Modification and Learning from Body Language and Environment.

How I Learned : the Value of "Adjusting"

By Bill Holmes

Most of us are fortunate enough to be born with the ability to leverage five senses as we navigate through life: Sight. Sound. Smell. Taste. Touch. Each sense works in coordination with the others. It is often said, in fact, that the loss of one heightens the power and sensitivity of those that remain.

From my point of view, one could also consider *speech* to be an important sense. Of course, you might reply that the power of speech is an "ability" and certainly it is. But speech is also the primary way we "sense" each other's thoughts and intentions.

At one point in my life I was temporarily deprived of the ability to speak. At another, I lost one of my five senses ... forever. The challenge of these two losses ultimately shaped me into the person I am today ... because both losses taught me the valuable lesson of learning to *adjust*.

I believe that humans, as a species, can learn to *adapt*. But individuals learn to *adjust*. But, it can take courage to adjust. It's a deeply personal decision. And sometimes adjusting means doing something that's "different" and goes against the norm.

I write this chapter to share these experiences, in hopes that what I've learned may be helpful to you. The lesson, in a nutshell, is about permanently maintaining a willingness and readiness to *adjust* in life i.e., adjusting to the unexpected by finding new solutions and opportunities that one would never have imagined otherwise. That idea is capsulized for me in this quote from Zig Ziglar, the American author, salesman, and motivational speaker:

"When obstacles arise,

you change your direction to reach your goal;

you do not change your decision to get there"

That is what life taught me: To remain open-minded enough to change my entire *direction* if I needed to do so I could then find, and mine, the silver in the lining of my cloud.

When I was in the seventh grade, I developed a throat infection, which led to a particularly bad case of laryngitis. But I was not prepared for what it led to: the complete *los*s of my ability to speak for an entire year!

Imagine a 13-year-old boy, just finding his balance while entering adolescence … discovering and establishing his new identity among family and friends, awkwardly navigating through the rapid and unpredictable onset of puberty and preparing for high school. And suddenly … unexpectedly … *he can't talk!*

I'd lost the sense, or the power, of normal and natural speech.

One of my strongest memories and motivators then was my 7th grade teacher, Pat Jennings. She understood what I was going through. She thoughtfully and supportively encouraged me to make adjustments in the classroom so that I wouldn't feel overlooked.

She sat me at the front of the room – visible to all. She would then call on me and make me recite, in a raspy gasp of breath, whatever lesson we were working on that day. I wasn't able to speak like the rest of my classmates but she made me learn to adjust and speak up – as best I could – anyway. Sadly, Pat is no longer with us. Before she passed, though, I was able to tell her how much her encouragement meant to me and how it positively impacted my life.

My voice eventually returned after speech therapy. The funny thing is that during the time that I couldn't speak, and unbeknownst to me, my pre-pubescent voice was secretly morphing into a deeper more masculine timbre. When I was able to talk again, the contrast with how I had spoken before was shocking! Some people actually imagined that somehow I'd been given artificial vocal chords.

During this time of silence, I remember inventing ways to compensate for my loss of speech. I still wanted and needed to express myself fully. To this day, I appreciate the impact we can have when we communicate only in silence. I would never have had that insight without my need to meet the challenge of being unable to speak.

Ultimately I regained my voice and went back to assuming that all would be "normal" in my life.

I've found that "adjusting" is not merely a coping mechanism but can also be a gift. Learning to see challenges as opportunities, too, has opened new doors I would never have thought to enter otherwise.

When I was growing up and challenges arose, my mother would always say, "The Will of God will never take you where the Grace of God cannot protect you". Looking back, I might have thought she meant that we should "roll with the punches." Or perhaps, "that which does not kill us makes us stronger."

I came to understand that what she meant was that we don't need to surrender ourselves abjectly to obstacles. Instead, I realize now, my mother wanted to reassure and inspire me ... into believing that whatever challenges I might face in my life ahead, they would also contain opportunities if I was sufficiently aware of the need to seek them. That take-away became a major lesson of my life, which I would like to offer to you now as I describe how I learned it.

Throughout my childhood and adolescence, all I ever aspired to be was a physician. My grandfather was a doctor and my father is a doctor. My uncles and cousins are doctors. That specific career was all I wanted and expected. I'd decided to become a surgeon and that was that!

When I was a junior in college I was preparing for the opportunity to apply to Medical School. I was working during the summers bartending at legendary Martin's Tavern in Georgetown, a suburb of Washington, D.C. One morning I woke up and knew immediately that something was different. I also sensed that something was very wrong.

After walking around a little, I found myself tripping over objects on the floor and bumping into tables and chairs. Soon it dawned on me that something was wrong with my vision. I began to experiment: Covering one eye at a time. It didn't take long to realize that most of my right eye's vision was gone. When I covered my left eye, I realized that I could only detect light in my right eye at the very top of my visual field.

I was frantic. I called my father back home in Pennsylvania. He urged me to visit the Georgetown University Hospital E.R. just as soon as I could get there. He thought I might be having some type of internal cerebral hemorrhage.

Many months and many trips to Will's Eye Hospital later ... and after many CAT scans and MRIs ... it was determined that I had developed optic neuritis. In other words, my vision loss would likely last for the rest of my life. I certainly hadn't seen *that* coming. My dream of becoming a surgeon came crashing to the ground – vision is *crucial* for that profession, of course.

I could have continued my goal of attending medical school and chosen another specialty. But as far as I was concerned at that moment, my dream was simply ... *over!* As I got older, though, I gained a valuable new piece of insight about this disappointment and others that had come my way. Still to this day, I use this insight as a guiding light as I journey forward:

It is not who we are in life that holds us back.

It is who we think that we are not.

I can't tell you how many times I have thought about the fact that, "I am not a doctor". As I mourned the loss of what had been my dream, I'd been ignoring potential opportunities by not considering what I *am* or what I *am* capable of.

While dealing with the shock of permanent loss of sight, I allowed this disability to became my self-definition. It was not until someone called me "handicapped", out loud, that I realized I had allowed myself to be defined by that problem instead of thinking of other ways that I could *define myself.*

I had been so wrapped up in the bitterness of feeling that something terrible had happened *to* me, that it was impossible at first to realize that something new and unexpected might have happened *for* me.

Please understand, this was not an epiphany happening in the moment. I knew that I always wanted to be a part of the healthcare industry ... and that I really could achieve that if I recognized the opportunities that were presenting themselves to me. With my vision loss, I couldn't be a surgeon but that didn't have to mean I couldn't find a *new* way to be in healthcare and feel the satisfaction that I felt I could only achieve by being a surgeon.

My initial ambition had stemmed, in part, from the admiration I felt for my father. I'd seen and been inspired by *his* dedication and the satisfaction he received from treating his patients. I wanted to be a part of that. I wanted to feel that same satisfaction.

Finally I realized that if I adjusted to the situation and proactively looked for ways to make it work – I *could* be part of healthcare. I *could* be part of improving patients' health.

After a few initial years in corporate life, I held several positions in the pharmaceutical marketing communications industry. I was involved in healthcare on a daily basis. And as I pursued my career, I found that I had become rather adept at adjusting to my environment and surroundings and some of my adjustments were subtle and known only to me.

For example, I made it a point to arrive *first* at any meeting. That way I could take the one o'clock seat at the conference table, which meant that the *only* person I couldn't directly see was the one to my immediate right.

If I was walking with someone, I quietly arranged that they would be on my left side, where I *could* keep them in sight.

Eventually, I realized that the only person that noticed that I had a sight loss was me! It simply didn't matter to anyone else. People felt comfortable with me when I was driving and I still had a pretty good tennis game. But there was one time during a doubles match when I didn't see my partner coming in to my right and I smacked him in the forehead with my racket in a forehand swing. (I'm sorry, Chris!)

The point is, my adjustments were both physical and psychological. Learning to make and even embrace them proved tremendously valuable because I was now open to the broader awareness that new perspectives could offer advantages and opportunities.

This core idea – the benefit of finding ways to adjust to reality and uncover hidden opportunities as a result – seems to be true for entire industries and organizations, as well. There has been more technological advancement in the last five years then there has in the last fifty. That advancement, and a business' ability, or inability and unwillingness, to adjust to these advancements has reshaped entire industries. We don't have to look too far back in history to see vivid examples of companies that did *not* adjust to the real and changing dynamics of their business landscapes.

Just consider …

Kodak – The inventor of modern film did not see the approaching juggernaut of the digital film industry. They were left behind forever in the digital stampede to the future.

Blockbuster – At one point, this former giant was in every strip mall in America and employed over 84,000 people worldwide until

Netflix disrupted their business model with the innovation of home delivery. Instead of ceding some of their profitability, Blockbuster filed for bankruptcy in 2004 and was eventually purchased by the Dish Network of satellites, another disruptor of the market.

Blackberry – The company whose name denoted an entire product category didn't adapt to the new world that Apple and Google were creating. Blackberry failed to see that it would be consumers – not businesses – who would drive the smart phone market. They lost customers by not adjusting to change.

Toys "R" Us – Saddled with crushing debt from a huge inventory and a glut of stores that couldn't move merchandise, for a long time this retail giant failed to see the transformational onslaught of online shopping from home. Their going-out-of-business liquidation sales began on March 23, 2018. Not adjusting can be fatal!

Now consider innovations that occurred almost by accident. Initially, when the original inventors didn't achieve what they'd hoped for, they persevered anyway adjusting their perspective in order to more clearly see the opportunities they'd actually created.

Think of the staples in our lives that wouldn't have been invented if the pioneers of these ideas had simply given up when results didn't match their expectations. Instead, they adapted their thinking and among the famous results in history are… Penicillin … Velcro … Post-It Notes…Viagra … Plastic … even Coca-Cola!

It was by recognizing the changes and adapting to them that I found a bit of a second career – focused on Learning and Performance Improvement. You could call that a form of "training" but I think there's much more to it.

I have come to believe that effective learning can be best expressed as building, through a continuum, one's ability to acquire knowledge, develop skill and sustain performance so as to effectively change behavior.

Isn't that what everyone really strives for? Whenever we read something, watch a video or take a course, our hope is that the information we take in will help us benefit from learning something new … and then applying it to our lives to create improvement.

We cannot adapt to reality, however, or find new opportunities within it, *unless* we pay attention to what reality puts in front of us. It is then up to us to adapt to the *Truths* we find. When we ask someone to pay "attention" to us we are asking them to give us something which has real value. We recognize the value of "attention" because it is emotional *currency*.

Over the course of the past few years I have written and developed several courses and I have been offered the opportunity to present these to audiences to share the insights that I have learned, intended to help others benefit from what life has taught me: *The Power of Paying Attention* and *Understanding and Reading Your Environment*.

It's always extremely gratifying when someone from one of my sessions tells me after the course that they will never look at a particular object, event or circumstance the same way again … because of the life lessons they learned while practicing the art of paying attention.

What I've experienced first-hand is the *power* that can come from being willing to adjust. Most importantly, it is essential that the judgments and the adjustments that we make are not driven by fear. Or by feeling that one is a "failure" because one couldn't achieve "X". Instead, it's very possible to discover what might be great – and even better – about opportunities "Y" and "Z" if our eyes are open to see them.

Uncertainty can be profoundly frightening, but the cost of giving in to fear is too high if we have not followed and trusted the instincts that guide us. We must allow ourselves to feel our own feelings. When we find ourselves facing a reality that disappoints us, it is essential that we never allow that disappointment to stop us from accepting reality and then being open and creative in adapting to it in new ways.

In short: "I learned to listen when I couldn't talk and I learned to observe when I couldn't see. I would never have learned either if I hadn't also embraced the need to **adjust** to the realities that confronted me."

I wish you the same creative and flexible mindset that has been so helpful to me ... so that you, too, are ready to adjust when you next encounter a reality that's different from what you'd hoped for or expected.

***

To Contact Bill

email: wjholmes5@gmail.com

LinkedIn: linkedin.com/in/bill-holmes-21361

Russell Reich

Russell is an experiential marketing executive based in New York and the publisher and co-author of all the books in the acclaimed *Notes On* series. He received Book of the Year honors from Foreword magazine and an Independent Publisher Award for *Notes on Directing*, a number one best-seller endorsed by Dame Judi Dench, Sir Ian McKellen, Sir Tom Stoppard, Sir Richard Eyre and three-time Pulitzer Prize winner, Edward Albee. Management expert Robert Sutton, writing for the *Harvard Business Review*, called it "One of my favorite books on the nitty-gritty of what wise bosses do." It was also named by the authors of *The 100 Best Business Books of All Time* as one of the three best books on leadership.

Russell's second book, *Notes on Cooking*, is endorsed by Jacques Pepin, Daniel Boulud, and five-time James Beard Award winner, James Peterson. *The New York Times* named it among "The Best of the Year." His 3rd and 4th fourth books (co-authored), *Notes on Teaching* and *128 Reflections*, appeared in 2011.

Russell served as a Visiting Artist-in-Residence at Harvard University and holds degrees from Colgate and Columbia Universities.

How to Get Any Job You Want

By Russell Reich

I lost my job.

Doesn't matter how or why. Perhaps I could have better positioned myself or better played my cards, but so what? Looking back doesn't make the slightest bit of difference to *what I do next*.

Besides, my particular circumstance has no relevance to *your* situation. I share my condition only to let you know that I know what it's like to be out of work and looking. And I want to let you know that even though I'm vulnerable not having work, I'm not *scared*. I'm actually confident and optimistic because of the information I'm about to share with you—three steps I'm using now and have used productively before. They work. I think they could help you, too, to ensure the best possible outcome to your own job search.

Fact is, at some point in our careers, we all find ourselves on the outside looking in.

Whether we're still in school seeking our first job, freshly graduated and looking for the start we don't yet know how to make, or suddenly out of work during mid- to late-career and needing a source of income, the job search is a common island on which nearly all of us find ourselves at one point or another.

Financially, we need to support ourselves as well as those we love while, hopefully, realizing some personal satisfaction, too. But being out of work is not only a threat to our financial well-being; it's also a challenge to our identity and self-image. When people ask, "what do you do?" or "where do you work?" they might as well be asking, "who are you?", "what are you?" and "what's your value to the rest of us?"

Being on the outside, without definition, is scary, and almost anyone can use some wise guidance on how to get "inside." So I'm here to do that, summarizing what I've learned for you and even for myself.

Not included are all the high-effort, low-result "front door" methods most people use that, *because* they come through the front door, make distinguishing yourself from the mob of applicants almost impossible. Instead, I will advocate for extremely self-directed, self-created *side door* opportunities to be recognized, seen, valued and hired.

Ready?

Step 1: Define Yourself and your Ideal Employer

If you don't know where you're going, any road will take you there. If you don't know what you want, why you want it, what you're good at, where your value lies, what you believe in, or where your talents are best applied, that doesn't mean you won't get a job. But you're more likely to be subject to someone else's idea of where you should be used, and at the lowest possible cost to them.

You don't want that.

Also, don't start with one of those "Best Companies to Work For" lists. That approach is too generic.

What does "best" mean, anyway, without any context of YOU and who you are. It means the general benefits and pay are probably good compared to others in the industry, or that the company has a good corporate responsibility profile or its own golf course, yadda-yadda. But "best" in such a general context tells you nothing about the potential for a specific spark that could really matter for YOU, one that could ignite between you and the right opportunity.

Just pursuing "best companies" from a list you find is like marrying someone because their family belongs to the right club, or roots for the right sports team—a nice alignment of interests, but hardly central to the task at hand.

Our kind of match-made-in-heaven possibility probably won't include any industry-leading, company-wide policy or benefit … because those things aren't central to a relationship based on substantial and specific *exchange of value*, which is what we're aiming for. A better approach would be first to **understand the value you represent to a potential employer … and then to seek out employers who need the value you can offer.**

In a way, you should be slightly inverting the "best" company approach by targeting a possibly *less*-than-best company, or even a slightly broken one … a place that really needs what you can offer. That's likely to come closer to being the Ideal Company *for you.*

So, again, first step: get a handle on what people would value in you—and what they'd pay you for.

Can you fix things? Can you write or speak especially well? Are you a good negotiator? Are you a leader people listen to? Do you have unique opinions and rare insights on your industry?

The possibilities for self-definition are wide but you need to be precise, VERY SPECIFIC and honest in assessing yourself based on evidence. If you're young and/or unformed, here are some quick ideas to help you get to your core:

What repeated and consistent praise have you heard from others?

If you had nothing to do, what would you *choose* to do? Build a drone? Write a book? Rebuild an engine? Start a club? Play with investments? Teach a class? Now: what are the component skills and sensibilities to doing well those things that you would choose for yourself?

Remember when you were in school? Can you think of an assignment that led other students to dive under their desks (writing a paper, field day competition, participating in a science fair...) but that made *you* light up with excitement and a sense of possibility?

Ask for help in defining yourself and in expressing that definition. Test your thoughts about yourself and the way you communicate them with people you trust ... people who know you.

Your central purpose here is to land on a succinct story about yourself: *This is what I do. This is how I do it and why. This is what I've accomplished with my skills.*

Note, too, that technological change is now so rapid that defining yourself in only one way, without mentioning alternate skills both digital and human... or without the key skill of being an agile learner who can adapt on the fly, which enables you to thrive in the midst of change ... will put you at a disadvantage.

So look for your own *yin* and *yang*—the *this* and the *that* within yourself—and be able to articulate the range of who you can be and what you can offer.

Next, find companies that need what you've got.

If you're really good at something, the evidence is especially obvious when others around you stink at it. So if you've assessed yourself properly, the absence of what you—specifically *you*—can offer should be easy to recognize.

It's pretty binary: either your sensibilities are present or they're not in your prospective employer's brand expressions, their products, their customer experience, their presence at trade shows—you're checking these out, right? Your sensibilities are also either present in an organization's processes or culture, or they're not.

Of course, your decision about which companies to target is affected by the extent to which you can know or gain *from the outside* this knowledge about your potential employer ... by studying their website, LinkedIn page, etc. And of course, researching through Google, Hoovers, and other sources.

A good internal indicator that you've landed on a candidate employer with promise is when you react with a genuinely felt, *I Can Help These People*. When you think, *They Need Me*, THAT is a good sign.

This is not to say that an employer that stinks at what you DON'T stink at is the whole picture. Not at all. It's not enough that you have incremental value to offer. *They* have to *want* what you can offer.

So look for some aspirational evidence that the brand or company seeks to improve in an area that's one of your strengths. For example, if they just established a new division in your specialty. Or if you detect an interest in the media coverage you find about them. If they need what you offer but don't want it, you'll be projecting your own movie but the potential employer won't have a screen on which to see it. When you find a place with both need and desire for what you offer: pretty good place to start.

Make your list of companies. What's your evidence they both need and want the value you represent? Your answer to those questions will be the foundation of how you'll answer every important question they'll have about you. Whether they ask them overtly or not, you'll have in mind, regardless, the wisdom of conveying your desirable traits in everything you say.

Step 2: Find your Insider

One of the worst parts of your outside status as a job searcher is your lack of visibility to what's happening inside. You submit a resume. What happened to it? Who knows? You had an interview you thought went well but never got a follow-up call or email, not to mention an actual offer. What happened? Black hole.

That's a really disadvantageous position to be in, and not at all suited to the seriousness of your task.

So before you throw your resume at a job opening with a company you believe wants and needs what you offer, do something else first. Find someone inside that company who will talk to you. You really need your own spy, source, and/or advocate on the inside to triangulate your relationship between you, them, and a third person: the one who is making the hiring decision.

Maybe you already know people there who can serve as your insider. Great. If not, hey what is LinkedIn for, anyway? What is leveraging your network for? This. Ask everyone you know who *they* know that works there. Get the introduction. Persist in your quest to get connected.

Next, get that inside person on the phone for 30 minutes. Book the time and tell them your story: what you're after and what you offer. Within that context, ask how best to pursue a job there. Share the ad for the position you're thinking of applying to, if you've got one.

If the social signals are right, invite this person to lunch instead of a 30-minute call. Face to face is better—so much more information is exchanged because it's not just coming in through your ears and theirs. You'll pick up essential visual, non-verbal cues that you can't get over the phone. And we all need to eat, so your self-interested reach-out to them and use of their time is balanced by an offer that is considerate of and generous towards them.

I'm a big believer in taking people to lunch; it's among the best $30 a job searcher can spend.

(Speaking of which, and only slightly tangentially, I once read an article discussing the perfect food to order at a business lunch. Something that raises no suspicions about you or your character, and is easy to eat without any high potential for mishap. What is it? An *omelette!*)

The right insider will be a gold mine. They'll tell you the company's big challenges and gaps (needs that you can fill). They'll let you know who the decision-maker is for the position you're targeting. (Someone whom you'll research online and maybe contact directly to distinguish yourself). Perhaps they'll also offer to recommend you directly to this person; a gold ring of an outcome to this conversation if ever there was one.

If not, they'll still be in a position to assess your skill set and how to position it to the company in a way that maximizes your value (so you'll know how to describe your value in the most relevant way.) They'll confirm or squash your preconceptions of the company (so you won't step into it with off-base opinions) and they'll help and allow you to sharpen your assumptions that are actually on-target. They'll tell you the right phrases and divisional names to use (so you'll sound like an insider.)

And when the process gets underway, they'll be your eyes and ears to tell you what's happening on the inside and make what's normally invisible to you, visible. That way you can intervene appropriately before the decision is made. Or at least know where you stand without wasting time fretting needlessly or reading things into the situation that simply aren't true.

When you land the job, you'll owe this person a dinner, if not a car.

Step 3: Crush that Big "But"

If you've defined yourself accurately and appealingly, targeted your companies effectively and procured an appropriate insider, it's only a matter of time before you'll get a coveted conversation chain started via phone and then in face-to-face interviews. Once you're on that track, there's another inevitability to the conversation that sounds like this:

You're terrific. You're wonderful.

Insights into Self-Empowerment

We'd like to hire you.

But...

This is the Big But. Following it can be: "you're overqualified," "you're underqualified," "we don't have an opening," "we don't have the budget," "we don't know where to put you." Or anything else.

This situation is so common, it's epidemic. And as weakening as it can feel to hear it in the moment, it can also be your most powerful opportunity. Be ready for it, because the moment you hear it, this is what you'll say:

> I understand completely.
>
> So let me make a proposal to you...
>
> [pause]
>
> Bring me on board anyway.
>
> Find a desk for me.
>
> For TWO WEEKS ONLY!
>
> Pay me some minimal stipend,
>
> say $_____ per week
>
> just so there's some representation
>
> of an exchange of value.
>
> Just so I can put food on the table.
>
> At the end of those two weeks,
>
> if I'm not everything you now think I am—
>
> if I don't provide the value we both project I will—
>
> I'll go away.

The Change[16]

> And you, in any case,
>
> will have gotten far more value
>
> by what I will have contributed
>
> than what you will actually have paid for.
>
> But ... at the end of those two weeks,
>
> if I AM everything you just said to me,
>
> we'll find a place for me here at a fair salary
>
> and we'll review that salary again three months later.
>
> So we'll both have layers of assurance
>
> that this is the right relationship.
>
> Game?

Ballsy, right? I first got this advice 25 years ago from a contact my aunt gave me when I was just starting out. It's criminal that I can't identify the wonderful guy, basically a stranger, who shared that strategy with me and to whom I'll forever be indebted. But at least I'm passing it along now to you ... in the hope it will help you as it's helped me. And will again.

I took the gentleman's advice and applied it after a summer of intense job searching and interviews. The moment I heard the Big But, I knew just what to do. My interviewer lit up with my moxie and polite refusal to take no for an answer.

That was the moment my career began. It didn't take two weeks to establish my value; it took the two minutes during which I proposed those two weeks.

Two days into that trial, it was apparent to everyone that I was going to stick around. Momentum is a powerful force, and once I was inside, it would take an uphill effort to get me out again. This in addition to the enthusiasm, effort and quality of what I worked hard to contribute during the trial period.

Of course, not everyone will respond as that interviewer did. But with those who don't, what does that indicate?

One possibility is that the praise expressed about you was not sincere; the Big But was just an excuse to reject you—an indication of a lack of seriousness.

Clarity has its benefits. Even a disappointment can be instructive. The other person's lack of response to your proposal might be an indication you're talking to the wrong person, someone without the authority to "bend the rules" in the way you suggested. Or the blank stare you receive might indicate a bureaucratic culture in which imaginative thinking and personal initiative isn't permitted. Ever. All of this and whatever else you learn by the response you get becomes valuable intelligence and insight for YOU to consider ... an indicator of what it might be like to work there.

Another possibility is that you'll get that two-week trial but not get to a job offer. Maybe you'll see things on the inside that lead you to run like the wind from that place. Or maybe they really don't have a budget for you, a desk or whatever.

Don't be bitter; you risked those two weeks by making your proposal. So what? There probably wouldn't have been a more productive way you could have spent those two weeks in your job search. Think of what you'll have learned from that "inside" experience ... the insights you'll have gained, the new connections, even the friendships you might have made.

At the very least, crushing the Big But marks the crush-*er* as a serious and imaginative person likely to be remembered at the right company for future opportunities if they arise. You can always loop back again, proactively, on your own when you're next looking.

So those are the three steps. I believe they can work for any persistent and conscientious job searcher. I know that they work and have worked for me.

Now please excuse me. I've got a job interview with my Ideal Company in a couple of hours.

***

To contact Russell

russellreich@me.com

845.461.8522

https://www.linkedin.com/in/russell-reich-8aa235/

Merrilee Sweeney

Merrilee Sweeney, host of 'The Merrilee Show," where she and her co-host have an impromptu conversation about relevant topics and offer a new perspective with love. Merrilee is the author of "The Game, Winning by Virtue One Move at a Time," where she simplifies life complexities by narrowing it down to a game. "But What if Men Were Different," is a webinar intended to guide men to a better understanding of what love is and is not by increasing their awareness of behavior. Her work as a thought leader, speaker, mentor, and author, has created an adoring following from those committed to her message of love. Whatever the question, love is the answer. Merrilee is the mother of four children; her life and inspiration to teach what love is to her three boys and only daughter. Merrilee's loving message gets to the heart of relationship communication. She helps countless people successfully work through their family affairs, business partnerships, divorce, parenting, self-worth, and purpose while guiding their spiritual development to build character. Her language is simple and easy to understand, while her parables encourage others to make necessary changes. Merrilee is the voice for change. Whatever the question, Love is the answer.

The Problem with Women

By Merrilee Sweeney

Dear Reader,

Please allow me to explain. It is not my intention to offend, or to judge; I'm simply making an observation. My ability to observe is imperative to what I do, then I proceed to love my way through it. As an author, teacher, and public speaker, my industry is personal development, with my focus on love. I teach people *how* to do it, how to *be* love. To love, one must master patience and have the discipline to both achieve and maintain generations of victory. Life is a game, and love is always the answer.

As an observer, it has been my experience whether personal or shared that the underlining problem with our success in any relationship is our ability to love. Love is the key to our success. It unlocks the beauty and abundance in everything. Love is the creator of all things good, beautiful, wise, powerful, and useful. So what is the problem with women? Women represent the beauty in the world. Like every flower, song, sunset and ocean breeze, she encompasses everything. God created woman as the most beautiful embodiment of nature. She's the sweet scent of an orange blossom in spring and a peaceful turning leaf in the fall. A woman is as warm as the sun, and as wicked as a thunderous, winter storm. Yes, she is as complex as the seasons, some stay hot and others are cold. Some women are perfectly tempered, it depends on what they were told. Like the seed of a rose, her ability to develop free and beautiful is her environment to which she was planted. Let us now take a look to see how our seed is growing…

There she is, born perfect and beautiful in every way. From the moment of conception her existence relies upon love energy in the environment she was created. Her cells of wellness are hinged on the care from another. She hears every sound, feels every emotion, and absorbs every substance her environment is exposed. She is the beneficiary for everything her mother imposes. On the day of her birth she continues to rely on the mercy, consideration, wisdom, awareness and care of those who surround her. Who she will be and what she will become depends on the love she gets from everyone.

The beauty of a women encompasses the worlds existence. She is the garden of amazing wonder. She's beautiful, emotional and complex with a heart infinite in all directions. From the moment of conception love is what she is, but who she will become depends on the love that nurtures her. But what if she has none?

To have a little girl all pretty in pigtails, fairytales and glitter, all dressed up bringing joy to the world that surrounds her. Her smile is infectious and her giggle too. She can't help but shine the love she was sent here to do. She's daddy's little princess and mommy's twin too. Her world is safe, and warm until the day when her heart is torn. Mom and dad are fighting but she doesn't know why. From the corner of the room she hears them shouting, afraid to come out, she sits alone crying. The door slams shut and her daddy is gone. Here comes her mom cleaning, pretending nothing is wrong. She watches her mother, tears rolling down her face. Her heart hurts to see her mother cry. Daddy is gone with no one left for mom. Why does daddy yell and call mommy names? What did we do to be left alone just you and I?

It's the first day of school and her daddy is late. The bell rings, her mom gives her a kiss and sends her on her way. Alone she sits away from the others, she's not comfortable with boys who pull at her pigtails. Stop she pleads, but the boys keep on teasing. After school she plays with her friends until it's time to be picked up by the babysitter. Her mom works two shifts to pay the bills. There's not much time to play with her mother, there's still too much to do before the day is through.

The Change[16]

The weekends come, it's her time with her dad. They sit on the couch and watch t.v., dad has a beer while she pretends to make him tea. Daddy do you want to play with me? No he says, daddy is busy, I'll play after I watch the game. The doorbell rings, who is this she says. "Come on in," *her dad says and asks if he would like a drink.*

"Sure," *his friend replies looking in the fridge.*

"Oops there's nothing left. Hey I'll be right back," *dad says, and leaves her in the care of his friend. The door closes and daddy is gone. Who is this man he left with me alone?*

"Hello" *he says,* "my name is Dan. May I have some tea?" *With her little girl smile she is delighted to play. She pretends to pour him his cup of tea.* "Come on over here and sit on my lap." *Hesitant she looks down, but in a moment he picks her up and brings her closer.* "Do you know who I am?" *he asks.* "I am a friend of your daddy's," *he says, while laying his hand on her leg. She's uncomfortable and tries to get off.* "Wait, where are you going?" *He grabs with both hands while trying to make her laugh. She squirms, attempting to get away but his hands are too big. He pulls her close with one hand between her legs and the other around her chest. She's scared. Just then the door knob turns and he lets go of her. She runs to her dad relieved to see him, but he doesn't notice what just happened. Instead he asks her to give his friend a beer. Nothing is said as her dad and his friend sit on the couch watching their game, drinking and shouting never paying attention to her. Without a word, dad takes her home to get ready for the week again. Nothing is ever mentioned about what happened. She didn't know how or what to say to her mother and was afraid to be the blame. The years go by, her mother starts to date, each one lasting for only a short time. Each the same story ending in heartache.* "Don't trust men," *her mother would say,* "all they want to do is get you in bed."

The years of disrespect from each man had taken a toll. How she missed hearing the joy of her mother's laughter, but her mother's words weighed heavy on her. She's now fifteen with boys interested in more than being a friend. I love you they would say followed by a kiss. Then it's straight to the back seat naked until the end. All she wanted was to be loved, but each time that boy would disappoint. He would say things that made her feel warm and fuzzy until he had what he wanted. Then without warning he would stop calling. She learned early on how valuable was her appearance, and so she started to work on it. With a little glamour she could have whoever she wanted if she wore the right thing. Her life became focused on the superficial. Her mother was right, they only wanted one thing. Over and over she hoped she would find a man that was different, but each time she would take a hit. Her heartache became her indifference. She needed protection from the abusive men, so she stopped being so trusting. From that moment on she knew it was up to her to be self-sufficient to provide whatever was needed. Her independence made her the leader.

Now grown up, she meets a man in college who is gentle and kind, appearing to treat her with honor. He doesn't pressure or try to control her, instead he cooperates and submits by letting her take the rein. She's independent and strong and would never let a man get in the way of all she had planned. She's become accustomed to the wings she's grown, making decisions on whatever she pleased. She took to him thinking this kind of love is easy. Yes, it was true. She was able to do whatever she wanted, however it was more than she ever considered. Her choices weren't fun, they became more like decisions, ones she would rather her husband be positioned. In addition to washing dishes and handling her business, she was calling the mechanic, the plumber, the banker and even his mother. No matter how she pleaded and cried, she just couldn't get him to do what was needed. She definitely was not his most cherished flower, instead she became his nagging mother. His stubborn

The Change[16]

complacency turned bitter toward her nagging. He looked at her with contempt as if she was to blame. It didn't take long for her to remember that it was her who was responsible for her own happiness.

On her own she's perfectly fine needing no help from anyone. She had no interest in raising a man, she'd rather sit alone with her independence in hand. Love she thought was an exaggerated plan, but deep down inside was a little voice saying someday she would meet the right man. As for now she would cast her line then throw him back once her meal was done. That worked for a while, enjoying her fun until her second husband came along. He was strong, independent, and could easily make a decision. He pursued her without hesitation. This one took care of everything. She rarely had to make a decision as he kept her busy with distractions and going fun places. They would meet new people and he would buy her trinkets to keep her satisfied. With another "I do," this one makes number two. She never thought it would happen, but to her surprise he appeared to be the one to make her happy. She submitted to him, giving up her independence, trusting to stay home and give him a family. Just like her mother, she worked day and night to make a nice home for them and their plus one. How she loved her little princess. It was just them two as daddy was busy, never having time for his family. The years pass and they grow apart. The days of her being cherished were only remnants of the memories found in her wedding book. Too many words left unsaid, they rarely talk and now they sleep in separate beds. Long past are the days of her independence. What would she do if she walked out to start a new? Her looks are not the same and it's been a long time since she's had to play the game. The thought is scary, but how long would she allow her daughter to witness the love that is so obviously missing? Again she decides to go it alone, this time with a daughter in tow. Remembering back when she was a child, she swore she would protect her little girl from the men who didn't have the character to keep their hands off of her. "My princess," she would say, "stay away from little boys, they only want one thing, and it's to get you in trouble."

She became very protective of her little girl. The fear of the possibility would take over her emotion. "Who are you talking to," she would continue to ask, not letting her daughter experience friends especially where boys were concerned. Her daughter grew weary of the control and instead of being careful she became resentful. She played with all the boys, giving her body carelessly just to feel loved and in control of her decisions. It didn't matter if all they wanted just one thing. "My mom doesn't understand" she thought, 'this life is for me. I'll learn as I go." Now the struggle was not about men at all, respect was the issue that wasn't being resolved. Contrary to her ego, her self-worth was deflating. She became less attractive no matter what she would wear, and the only men interested in dating her were the ones who had no intention of marrying her. Her mother stood by as she watched her little girl go through the heartache and breakup, as each man failed to have the ability to love her without condition.

Are you starting to recognize the problem with women? What happened to the beautiful little girl so full of life, innocence and wonder? What happened to the little girl born to be a rose but instead grew into a thorn? Women of all ages suffer from the same dilemma. Regardless of her color, race, religion, origin, ancestry, name, orientation, success, style, or form, a woman is a woman and ought not to be treated like anything other. Although she may be resilient to lots of abuse, capable of managing her business, and adapt to her surroundings despite what is wrong, her true beauty and essence, is the authentic feminine spirit of love that can only be experienced when her environment nurtures her to become the love she was born. The delight of lightheartedness, creative, free-spirit is heard in her laughter when she's being respected. If the conditions fail, the result is pain, the same as we see in the world with each generation.

The Change[16]

Women are the heart of the world; broken with no one seeming to know how to repair it. What makes a women talk about another, and why do they scorn and complain to each other? Why do they suffer from a lack of self-confidence, crying in their room because nobody loves them? What has taken away their beauty? Maybe it's the keeper of her garden, because he doesn't know how to make her flower? Who is the keeper of the Garden? Men. It's a man who will till and nurture the soil. It's his duty to be a leader, so she is free to be the love of the land. Men are the leaders, protectors, and providers. When a man doesn't lead, who is left? She is. When a woman has to take over, she's robbed of her duty to be the sweet intoxicating scent a man is motivated to want more of. Instead he has created another leader to which he has no interest. Once he has failed to be all that he can be, she naturally steps in but not without sacrificing a piece of her dignity. Equality they say, let a woman be the same. Give her the opportunity to fend for herself. Why can't she do it they complain while stepping back and allowing her to pay. The condition of a woman has been diminished in so many ways. So often she's expected to please him, objectified to increase his self-worth. Back at home he's done for the night, never giving her what she needs to replenish the love she has for him.

She is his treasure, giving birth to his children. Unfortunately, her body makes changes, now he becomes disinterested. What does she have left to give? Only the love she has for her kids. He doesn't understand, the attractive garden he once had has now been lost by the carelessness of his own hand. A man often doesn't realize his lack of understanding, to care for his garden requires him to grow into a multi-faceted man. What a plight of despair that these men have been raised by the same women who've been hurt, abused and disappointed by leaders along the way. But what if men were different? How would the world be if men understood how to care for their women? What would it look like and how would they be?

First let's look at the symptoms of the disease. She makes allowances for all that is missing, and instead holds on to the idea that he will serve good enough for his purpose. She rather not be alone, spending everyday with him although wishing he were more loving, attentive, and aware. She's hurting but he does not see, the injury so apparent in her self-esteem. She looks to him for safe refuge, but instead he continues to put her down and disrespect her every effort to be the woman she so longs to be. His voice so powerful, if only he could see, to make her bloom, he needs to sing music to her ears. No, instead the pain of his own heart is spoken without care. Why he hurting? She doesn't know. It's not easy being a man. Who is teaching him how? It's not her job to show him what to do, so who is left, where can he go? He is expected just to know. It's not enough to be intelligent, handsome, funny, or well spoken. Who is responsible to teach him the complexity of love in the Garden? He's followed the system to the best of his knowledge, going to church, paying the bills, and marrying the girl that gave him a child. 'Who is paying attention?' he might think, but looking around there are many problems in this world.

Who is to blame, and where can we point the finger? There are only two genders, each with one role. If men were different, and could understand what they were doing, maybe then women would be free to bloom in her place, beautiful just being.

To understand the complexity of a woman, one must first understand love. Love is the key to unlock everything. The result of his understanding is the polished man God created in him. God only knows the road he will take, but as long as he makes the Most High his dwelling, the Kingdom of Heaven will honor his efforts. Back to the Garden the world will follow... if only a man would have the courage and humility to be different.

Merrilee Sweeney

Honor is a word so few illustrate. Depending on one's behavior it can be lost in an instant.

It takes the mastery of patience and discipline to both achieve and maintain generations of victory.

***

To Contact Merrilee:

themerrileeshow.com

butwhatifmenweredifferent.com

www.facebook.com/merrileekleinsweeney

www.facebook.com/TheMerrileeShow

https://www.youtube.com/channel/UCEi0hjXmOhS43NiV3adnEKg

Phil Bristol

Phil Bristol, the Founder, President and CEO of Projectivity Solutions, integrates 130 years of business, organizational development, and people skills research into each engagement. He works with boards of directors, executives, leaders, high-potentials and teams to increase their effectiveness, influence and profitability. He helps facilitate personal and organizational change, serves as a sounding board on complex people issues and works with top performers so they advance to the next level of responsibility. Projectivity Solutions, Inc. helps businesses increase growth and profitability while solving the multi-generation challenge of family owned businesses. Facilitated solutions help owners develop and communicate a customized "Gold Standard" that creates and sustains a culture trust-based high performance. Phil is passionate about helping people and organizations move to new levels on their journey. In doing this, he uses his practical business techniques and tools, expertise in interpersonal skills, communication, critical thinking, business strategy and execution to produce pragmatic results that helps move individuals and organizations to the next level of performance. He is an entrepreneur and leader with over 35 years of business experience and has run a successful company for over 25 years. His presentations and workshops are acclaimed by executives worldwide.

Don't Let the Family Drama Vortex Shatter Your Family Business Legacy

By Phil Bristol

The Greatest Economic Engine Faces the Greatest Challenges.

There are 29 million small businesses in the U.S., and they account for 99.7% of the economy, 60% of employment and 78% of new jobs. And for all business, family owned businesses account for over 50% of U.S. GNP. That's the good news.

Here's the bad news – 70% of family owned businesses only survive one generation. And while 30% make it to a second, only 10-15% make it to a third, and a miniscule 3-5% make it to a fourth generation. So why are family owned business so vexed to succeed as multi-generational enterprises? The answer is simple. While it's hard enough to work with co-workers and colleagues, it is exponentially more difficult working with family members and all the relationship baggage. An additional complication is the overlap of family, business and ownership roles. Amplifying these challenges are non-existent skills to create trust based communication, lead with influence, and clarify expectations. These hidden forces condemn most family owned businesses to a one generation life-cycle. Now consider just how our economy, not to mention the individual success of your family owned business, would benefit by solving these challenges. Overcoming these unique family business challenges will restore harmony, create a lasting competitive advantage, and unite generations.

Restoring the Harmony in Multi-Generation Family Owned Businesses

A multi-generation family owned business typically begins because of the founder's passion and entrepreneurial spirit, and then grows organically with increased customer demand. But family business founders are too often so passionate about working in-the-business that they become distracted from working on-the-business. The result is that they become unaware of naturally occurring conflicts that arise. Over time, this nearsighted focus leaves business, ownership and family issues unresolved. Your business may be teetering on the edge of this "Growth Abyss". And when it occurs you are sucked into the *Family Drama Vortex* and vulnerable to years of people conflict which can shatter the business legacy.

Is the Legacy of Your Family Owned Business Threatened... by Family?

Family owned businesses face a unique set of challenges that can threaten the existence of the business by virtue of being *family owned*. You must grapple with all the traditional business challenges, but also face the additional challenges associated with family dynamics that can damage both relationships and the family business legacy.

At the core of this dilemma is the fact that it is simply not possible to separate or ignore the collision and friction that occurs when you overlap business, ownership and family... *among family members.*

The result is dysfunction and paralysis within the business as competing needs fracture family members into tribes that advocate for their path and generate roadblocks for others. Everyone talks about the problems, but nothing gets resolved because relationship factions paralyze the capacity to work *on the business.*

Further alienating the factions and entrenching separate positions is the continued Tribal Chant of "do it my way" from the founder. The result is that existing problems don't get resolved and new problems just go on the "to do list". The business lurches forward and nothing gets resolved.

As the business grows leaders attempt to solve the growing complexities and challenges by adding people. Adding more people without solving the underlying business and family issues only makes the problem worse. Over time, accumulated problems diminish business functionality and further fuel family member issues that are affecting the business. At some point, the legacy of the family business is in jeopardy of survival.

Is Your Business Teetering into the Growth Abyss?

Family owned businesses follow a predicable trajectory. The founder is an entrepreneur with the belief that hard work fosters success. The business is born with a few family members or close associates. In the early stages communication is easy because there are few people and the relationships are long-term. But as the business grows the founder needs help. The obvious solution is to bring on other family and close associates. This is the beginning of the all-consuming problems associated with the collision of overlapping roles, responsibilities, needs, wants, desires and personal baggage of family members endeavoring to work together.

Bringing in family members, rather than solving problems, is a trap because it inextricably entangles the business in a litany of issues including long standing grudges, unresolved wounds and lack of trust between family members, plus poor conflict resolution skills and the inherent behavioral dysfunctions permeating family relationships. Complicating matters is the natural behavior of family members to actively seek others as allies to their particular viewpoint. This creates separate and competing voices that distract and challenge that of others in the business.

As chaos grows and productivity is challenged the founder tries to rein in the mayhem by demanding "do it my way". This "Tribal Chant" works in the beginning but it fails as the business grows and more people are added. That's because Tribal Chant is not effective communication in complex organizations. Adding more people only increases the distracting relationship collusions that further pushes the business into the growth abyss.

Written Documentation Transcends Tribal Chant

Dropping into the growth abyss is avoidable by using written artifacts to clearly articulate three critical elements of culture, business direction, work expectations, and relationship expectations. Written artifacts clarify expectations not only on the "what" and "how", but also ensures consistent and verifiable communication throughout the organization. As such, written artifacts replace Tribal Chant by providing clarity on work execution and guidance on how we will treat each other.

Without this clarity, productivity and profitability does not improve regardless of how much the founder rants "do it my way". Chaos ensues, collusion runs rampant, and Tribal Chant becomes the culture of how people treat each other. Ambiguity and uncertainty spreads throughout the organization, while family dynamics, permeates the business with inter-personal turmoil, for which neither the founder nor the family members are prepared.

Unfortunately, most founders are not innately prepared with the knowledge, skill sets, or expertise to openly implement the three elements of success, let alone document them in written artifacts. So founders do what they think is best - add more family and continue to chant "do it my way".

What's Unique About Family-Owned Businesses: Family Drama?

Family-owned businesses lack the veil of civility that exists in non-family owned businesses. Family members act in ways that others would never do in other businesses. Lack of civility exacerbates problems because relationships and work complexities dramatically increase as people are added to the business.

Adding more people creates an exponential number of inter-personal relationships where the "family drama" magnifies and the number of "chaos interactions" increase. This opens the door to intense communication and leadership challenges. Adding to the chaos is the overlap of "owner", "family" and "employee" roles and responsibilities that without proper boundaries will result in abuse, negligence and misuse of roles and relationships, and intensify member rivalries and conflicts. It is this ambiguity between "owner", "family" and "employee" roles which allows members to inappropriately act and speak as if entitled.

As the business grows, these contentious family dynamics inhibit the ability of business leaders to effectively manage the normal challenges of growth. Unresolved family challenges stack up and intensify, business dysfunction intensifies, and underlying issues create turmoil. This paralyzes the ability to work on the business.

We Call This the Family Drama Vortex

In this culture of chaos, the only focus is to just survive. The attitude becomes "me-centric", a mindset that together with underlying family dynamic issues, results in what we call *The Family Drama Vortex* - the spiraling, recurring series of negative, emotional, distracting and damaging interactions among family members. The problem is compounded by normal business challenges and the inability of family members to effectively work on resolving business issues. As the vortex spins, personal baggage intensifies "me-centric thinking" further increasing isolation. The result is that barriers are created, nothing gets resolved and success is threatened.

When you're consumed by the vortex, you're not able to accurately assess your current business situation and it becomes virtually impossible to recognize or work on the three critical "elements" that will successfully move your business forward – *profits, people and process*. It also has the potential to destroy relations.

Signs that your business is affected by the drama vortex may include family members wanting out, eroding profits, financial stress from poor cash flow, worsening employee issues, unplanned departures, collapsing moral, and workplace incidents causing increased medical cost.

An owner cannot ignore the possibility that the wrong people are doing the wrong jobs, and the way employees are treated has resulted in a dramatic drop of productivity and quality or loss of customers.

The personal impact to family members can range from harmful to potentially devastating. Common realities include in-fighting between family members, verbal assaults, fights, combative interactions, hurt feelings, estrangement, ruined holidays and events, damaged relationships, divorce, health issues, loss of engagement, isolation, substance abuse, inappropriate entitlement and unreasonable expectations for next generations.

Communication is at the Root of Taming the Family Drama Vortex

The core solution for addressing the Family Drama Vortex is understanding that the drama and dysfunction is rooted in communication and interpersonal skills. Only when leaders, team and family members communicate in a way that disarms me-centric behavior, acknowledges challenges and creates an environment for openness and understanding, are family and team members then able to realistically discuss and solve business issues.

Effective conversations begin when leaders and team members recognize the nature of how they are currently communicating, and how their actions impact outcomes and relationships (i.e. how we speak and hear). During early business stages, "do it my way" is appropriate as this dominate style provides the necessary information on what needs to be accomplished to achieve needed results.

But over time this "I'm right... do it my way" style of communication becomes mirrored by others, especially family members with the cumulative effect that essential business challenges are not addressed, functional silos begin to form and business and personal barriers begin to build.

The Way You Communicate Matters

Understand that word choices, tone, and patterns with which we speak effects what others hear. The result is that when a family member hears (perceives) that their role, responsibilities, wants, or desires have been threatened, the response will likely be out-of-balance, inappropriate, or confrontational. The ensuing conversation will have nothing to do with addressing a business challenge, but have everything to do with fueling the tension.

The solution is to "unpack the process", dissembling how and why family members are interacting, and incrementally moving individuals and tribes from a low-trust to a high-trust culture. Unpacking is not just about managing or resolving conflict, but about transforming trust-based relationships. In the end, untangling family member dysfunctional interactions helps reveal why and how we communicate, acknowledges the family dynamic issues between members, and ultimately increasing how we interact and trust.

A Place for Leadership

The leadership style of "do it my way" fails at problem solving as the business grows. People don't like management by force. Family and other members comply by doing what they are told, but they do not commit. Compliance is a mode of stopping the yelling, but it creates resentment and dissention. The underlying discord is: "I'll do it to shut you up, but not because I care!" Management by nagging prevents achieving long lasting results. But unfortunately this is the common evolution of a family owned business. The fundamental problem is that founders are often un-equipped for the stages of leadership required to move beyond "my way works" and truly motivate a team to care, follow and excel.

Without the required interpersonal skills mindset, founders are challenged to recognize the changes in business and family dynamics and are unequipped to adjust their leadership style to effect the real change needed by the team and organization. This becomes a severe problem with increased staffing levels.

But with the required skill set, leadership can move towards motivating and inspiring others. This comes from appropriate communication and a focus on cohesive efforts to produce results. Leadership moves from "my way works" to communicating clarity of direction, clarity of work expectations and clarity of relationship expectations.

Our Approach in Helping Family Owned Businesses Succeed

The *Family Drama Vortex* can be stopped. Meaningful transformation begins when family members recognize the drama vortex signs and become alive to the collateral damage imposed upon the family and the business.

We use proprietary tools and methods to restructure communication and clarify family-business roles and responsibilities. At the same time, we also focus on family and business issues, developing the communication and other skills within family members so they can effectively work on the business.

This consultant-facilitated approach helps put the vortex forces in check and allows family members to prioritize the essential activities inherent in a successful business – planning, finance, human resources, marketing and sales and innovation (i.e. the elements of profits, people and process).

We begin by addressing family drama, getting members to recognize situational clues and symptoms. Then we help family members enhance their skills to appropriately communicate, interact and work with others in the business. In tandem, we help each family member determine their "right fit" for business roles and responsibilities.

At the same time, we assess and prioritize core business challenges, develop solutions, and then deliver a custom set of tools to build into business practices to make implemented solutions self-sustaining. As a business adds people and grows in complexity, an owner's focus is always on profit, process, and people. We help executives determine which of the three needs the most attention for each unique stage of business maturity. For relationships, the primary focus is always on building trust, managing conflict and establishing accountability.

Our five step roadmap to business success, is a progressive, collaborative process to identify the critical business performance issues. Designed to discover right-fit solutions and address core issues, this is on-going continuous business improvement cycle. The five step roadmap removes the Family Drama Vortex as a roadblock to success and builds a lasting competitive advantage.

Discovery – A confidential, initial consultation to collect symptoms, clarify desired outcomes, determine obstacles to success and gauge likelihood of success. This results in an objective business and team performance review using a set of proven diagnostic tools to identify the most critical needs for the business.

Realignment – Use the diagnostic results to co-create a detailed implementation plan linked to strategic results. The purpose is to help the senior leadership team rediscover/refocus on a shared understanding of the organization's potential. This helps re-establish individual, employee and business alignment that is committed to, and accountable for, targeted results.

Implementation – First secure leadership agreement on the "Key Result Indicators" needed to track and measure progress. Then prioritize desired results with leadership alignment on the single most important outcome and the two-three supporting results needed to stabilize and move the business forward. Next is the development of simple implementation plans with clear accountability, including accountability meetings. The overall goal is to identify and build on current success with brand, leadership and culture.

Validation – Firmly and deeply establish customized best practices into the DNA of the business and leadership though individual and team coaching. That means building internal capability for sustaining conversations, growth plans and alignment across the organization.

Evolution – Cascade and infuse efforts throughout the organization and solidify this new foundation for successfully moving their business forward. This is also evaluation of the engagement's goals and activity achievements as measured against traditional business metrics and client satisfaction

The five step roadmap consolidates and documents the three "clarity" requirements, plans, process, and people. Owners document where the organization is going, the expectations for customer engagement and service quality, and how people will be treated. Concurrently, we take a comprehensive approach to addressing family-business related roles, responsibilities and issues by integrating a process called "The Family Council" into an engagement. The Family Council is an opportunity for all generations of the family to meet, discuss, communicate and pull together on issues affecting business, ownership and family – the triad of a family owned business.

Measuring Success

Ultimate business success is measured by profits. But profits alone are not sustainable without productivity, which is not sustainable without having the right people, in the right position, communicating and working as a team. So the simple goal of maximizing profits is not the best measure of sustainable financial success. In our engagement, success is measured by improved communication, acknowledged understanding on the part of individual family members, ability to discuss and resolve business issues, incremental restructuring of members into appropriate roles and responsibilities, organizational cultural change and improved business health. Succinctly, we measure our success by the positive impact we have on your business.

Our Approach and Philosophy

We advocate that a company culture where leaders influence and inspire their team to produce quality results and sustain trust-based relationships thrives and creates a lasting competitive advantage. The core proposition is that there is a demonstrated relationship between how managers treat employees and a company's lasting competitive advantage. The challenge is that managing people, sustaining a trust-based culture, and developing interpersonal skills are the least developed competencies for leaders and managers. Without the right interpersonal skills, a leader's capacity to confront difficult situations and the pressure to provide quick results will most likely undermine quality, client satisfaction, and employee enthusiastic commitment.

We help multi-generation family owned businesses identify which cultural factors are creating the most drag on productivity and profit, and then help develop cost-effective solutions that will yield a high return on your investment. This includes an examination of how leaders, managers, family members and employees are treating each other, and working to develop the interpersonal skills to create and sustain trust and respect between the players in the business.

Final Thoughts

Projectivity Solutions, Inc. helps businesses increase growth and profitability by demonstrating to executives that great financial rewards come from living up to the high standards that most businesses advocate, but few achieve. Solving the multi-generation challenge creates a trust-based, high-performance culture which has clarity of direction, work expectations and relationship expectations for a lasting competitive advantage and family legacy.

***

To contact Phil:

Projectivity Solutions, Inc.

866.350.0707 Toll-Free

866.445.4973 Fax

916.346.5033 Mobile

www.projectivity-solutions.com

Stacey Cargnelutti

As an International Best Selling Author of the book series 'Living Without Limitations,' a Life, Faith & Fitness Coach, and Creator of 'P3 – The Perfect Workout,' Stacey shares her passion for inspired, fit living, worldwide. She educates, inspires and empowers. Her ways provoke thought and help many make the transition from rough, stormy seas, to beautiful, calm sandy beaches. Her desire is to help you experience greater levels of grace and glory as you live out your destined purpose with passion.

Stacey is a seasoned, group exercise veteran with over 35 years of experience in the trenches of the fitness industry. She has designed and implemented award winning fitness programs and worked with every age while touching all with her positive, contagious energy, and spirit led life.

Her belief that 'meaningful connection is the key to lasting change and sustained motivation' is authentic, and lived out in all she does. Stacey puts the heart and soul back into fitness and is an inspiration to life itself!

She's a true Agent of Change. Her work empowers all to live higher, go deeper and reach beyond... She uses a blend of word therapy, inspired action, and lots of love to confront complacency and help you reclaim your life and future.

Stacey's heart for people, as well as her passion, enthusiasm, and wisdom, testify of the great wealth of true and total health. May her work inspire you to a prosperous life of divine intimacy, action and impact!

From Faith to Fitness

By Stacey Cargnelutti

"Eat clean and exercise." It sounds easy enough. Ya? Why then the rising epidemic of obesity, the ramped body shame, and the increase in lifestyle-related disease?

Although training methods are 'backed by research,' and people are losing millions of pounds around the globe, few stories end in the lasting change hoped for. The truth is, body transformation as any transformation, comes by faith. Apart from a relevant, meaningful, divine connection, mankind's fuel tank runs dry.

Fitness is nothing more than a state of preparedness that equips one to be ready in season and out, to go, do and be, without hindrance or limitation. To be fit is to function according to divine design and sustain homeostasis at higher and higher levels of output and intensity. When the spirit, soul and body align, peace guides, love compels, joy strengthens and fitness flows.

Harmony is a 'congruent arrangement of parts,' the working out of truth. It is real and powerful because it flows only from enlightenment that produces integrity and sincerity. It's the evidence of an authentic connection to personal values, deep seeded convictions and God Himself. Harmony is spiritual in nature and plays a vital role in the development and maintenance of overall fitness.

Although few argue that faith is the path to ruling and reigning in life, faith-based programming is rarely given a serious platform due to its spiritual and immeasurable nature.

"Faith is the substance of things hoped for and the evidence of things unseen." (Hebrews 11:1)

A measure of faith is given to all. This invisible substance is the divine agent for change and the evidence that you already have what you're hoping for. Faith is energy! It is alive and active and confirmed by corresponding action. When you take a risk and receive the 'anointed utterance' or inspired word and make the choice to believe in what you cannot yet see, your spirit jumps for joy at helping you unleash yourself, live in love, and soar!

The following faith-based programming keys are based on the premise that you are created in the image and likeness of God. You are a speaking spirit, you live in a body, and you have a soul that houses your mind, will, and emotions.

1. Who you are determines what you do.

Defining and connecting with your true identity is always the first step in making positive change. Athletes train, champions win, writers write, and those believing they are healed and victorious align their lives with health and victory. So before we go any further, 'Who do you say you are?' Close your eyes for a moment and imagine you at your very best. How do you look, feel, think, speak, decide, act, and move? This is the real you.

In seeing yourself strong, determined, well-able, and fully equipped, you begin to take on this identity in thought, word and deed. Soon you are manifesting the true you. And when you are ready to see more and get even greater results, you will open up your spiritual eyes and embrace more of the greatness seeded within.

"It is no longer I who live but Christ who lives in me…" Galatians 2:20

Contained in this one revelation is unlimited power and potential, and tremendous intrinsic motivation! When you believe that you are, you will be, and therefore do.

2. Real and lasting change is spiritual and happens in the context of relationship.

Did you know that your drive for connection is greater than your drive for food? You are a relational being. "It is not good that mankind be alone…" God said, "I will make him a helper suitable." I believe social media has given us some pretty good evidence regarding our need for connection even in the shallows of life, but when it comes to making lasting change, deep, meaningful connection with God and others is vital. This is why God calls us to Himself and not to morality, mental ascension or religious ritual. Spiritual consciousness, godly character, and personal power are the evidence of divine connection and not the means to acquiring it.

Because you are a triune being created in the image and likeness of God, your body, soul (mind, will, emotions), and spirit fail to function optimally independent of one another. Disorder, misalignment and disconnect radically effect performance and function. Can you imagine the chaos that reigns when your spirit nods off and neglects its role of leadership? Of course the body and soul are ready and willing to 'step up,' but neither is designed to lead and therefore they lack the equipping and grace to be effective.

The body and soul are responders. They make decisions based on past experience, safety and comfort, vs. wisdom and integrity. Their leadership results in powerless sensuality and egocentric narcissism. Beware!

Your awakened spirit holds the power to give you the body of your dreams and all other desires of your heart. According to divine design, the chain of command is as follows: Spirit. Soul. Body. Your body is subject to you, not you to it. Allowing it to usurp will disqualify you from the race and life is not a spectator sport! You are in it to win it!

Man's spirit is called the 'lamp of the Lord' because it holds the thoughts, feelings and intentions of God's heart and illuminates paths of righteousness so you can know and enjoy life to the full. Spirit-led living is the path to honor, power and glory.

God's deep desire is YOU. And secondly, that you experience the power of divine intimacy. The unforced rhythms of grace that flow from the heart of God through the conduit of meaningful and divine romance are for the purpose of ushering mankind into the power and glory he is designed to know and in so knowing, bring heaven to earth.

Love compels, restrains, expresses itself and changes all it touches including your body. Transformation flows freely in love and becomes purposeful in fulfilling the plan of God for your life. Sustaining love is to sustain MOJO! Knowing that you are from love, sustained by love, and purposed for love, is the realization that empowers you to conquer all. You are a force to be reckoned with but if you don't 'deep down know it,' you will lack confidence, direction and motivation.

Disconnecting any area of your life from your essence of love is to unplug from your fuel source, lose power, and 'die.' Burn out happens to those living in the realm of the natural. Attempting body transformation apart from a spirit to Spirit connection is to 'run the car on three cylinders instead of four' and forfeit great power.

3. All you need is desire and oxygen.

God's words are the truest expression of the real you. They reveal your deepest needs and unveil your deepest desires. "Delight yourself in the Lord and He'll give you the desires of your heart." (Psalm 37:4) Your desire is a prophetic picture of God's perfect will for your life. Few are skilled at identifying their desires because they mistake desire for controlling lust and identify with their sinful, sensual nature more than their redeemed, true and divine nature. It takes the brutal honesty, supreme wisdom and supernatural power of intimacy with God, to align your intentions with your actions.

We fight and quarrel because our passions and desires war within us; we don't have what we want. And although we may ask, we ask for the wrong things.

The blueprint for your best body is in your spirit. Your life as well as your body, is hidden with Christ in God, which means He is the way to attaining health, strength and weight loss. All these things are worked out of you by grace through faith in the realm of the spirit as you renew your mind and abide in truth.

When desire has its rightful way, your life and the 'blueprint' match. This place of harmony aligns you with the abundant life you are designed and destined for. It's a place of no compromise, complacency, and burn out because none of these exist in the spirit. To live in alignment with your true self is to know the wealth of health as well as the power to sustain it. Once you taste the bliss and high energy of connecting with your source of inspiration and living out your intentions, all else pales and your tolerance for compromise will cease.

To ignite the 'fire of desire' needed to fuel your change, ask yourself, "Who am I and what do I look, feel and move like?"

What does a fit body give you? How does this fit body fulfill your deepest needs of certainty, variety, significance, connection, contribution, growth, and creativity?

Your reasons for doing the work of body transformation need to be compelling! They need to inspire and move you into action and produce results that last. Hiring a 'pusher' will buy you some time, but sooner or later it comes back to you and your desire for change.

Relevant, living faith is the oxygen that fuels your desire and inspires you to take action toward it. Reading the inspired words, listening to stories of transformation, observing lifestyles you can appreciate, developing character, and doing what you respect others for doing, are a few ways to stay aligned with your God-given desires.

It's the fire that burns off the dross, lightens the load, illuminates the path, and moves you in heart-centered ways. Desire is a powerful grace intended to move you onward and upward in good and godly directions of love, life, health, peace, power and joy and bring you into perfect harmonic flow; spirit, soul, body.

4. Nothing happens until something moves.

Because the words of God are alive and active, they work in you 'both to will and to do.' And because they are spirit, they quicken your physical body and move you into action. Your spirit has been appointed the job of leadership and when it's given authority, it empowers you in transcending human expectation! The more time you spend in the word of God the more harmony and resurrection power you will operate in and know.

Just as your natural body was formed from the dust of the ground and requires natural substance to sustain life and growth, so your spirit was formed of Spirit and requires spiritual food to sustain life and growth. The words of God are spirit, truth and life. They set you free to show up in full power and presence and reclaim your life.

Not only is faith your true fuel supply but it's also the mirror that reveals the real you. You are not to wait for heaven to enjoy the freedom and power of abundant life, your inheritance of authority, health, hope, wholeness, light, wisdom, love… is for now. Your mission and mandate is to bring heaven to earth.

As the incorruptible, spiritual seed of the word manifests, the person, life, and power of Christ is revealed to and through you. When He appears, the sobering realization that you are 'like Him' begins to have its life-changing way in your heart and you become unstoppable! Soon, the glory given you begins to touch the world in naturally, supernatural ways. (1 John 3:2, John 17:22)

As I mentioned earlier, your physical body is subject to you according to divine order. Keep it under you! One of the biggest mistakes we make is giving authority to the body and soul by subjecting ourselves to inferior mindsets that lead us to the pantry and couch rather than the juice bar or gym. Exercise produces profit because it requires you to do the hard thing by sowing to the spirit and growing the inner man rather than giving preference to comfort and ease, sowing to the flesh, and reaping destruction.

Every new move of God begins with a new sound. Worshipers led troops into battle, walls fell down with a shout, and no one crosses a finish line alone. Victory has a voice! This may sound a bit weird but your throat is really a birth canal for 'spiritual babies.' Meaning, nothing happens that hasn't first been spoken.

A friend of mine described the wall she hit at mile twelve of a half marathon she was running. As fatigue set in a voice from the sideline shouted, "Go Laura! You got this!!!" It was the word she needed to inspire her last mile and finish her race.

Both life and death are in the power of the tongue, angels move to accomplish the will of God when they hear a voice of truth, and demons move to execute evil when they hear perversity (words contrary to the will of God). Your words move heaven and hell and attach meaning and emotion (energy in motion) to everything. They are the literal substance creating peace, bringing joy, building bodies, strengthening relationships or destroying everything; you decide. Your tongue unleashes great power in your life and on the earth.

As the leader of your life, can you detect areas of misalignment? Speak order over the chaos. Just as God saw darkness and said, "Let there be light" you are designed to 'call those things that are not as though they are.' Call your body "healthy, strong, slim, fit, and able…" There is grace in the spoken word that longs to work on your behalf. In Genesis 1 we find God's 'formula' for creation… "God said…, and it was so." When you believe that what you say is coming your way, your thoughts, feelings, words and ways will begin to align with your desires and manifest abundant life. God spoke and 'it was,' time and again because nothing within Him resisted. His whole being was in harmony and not at war within itself.

In what areas are you living contrary to your intentions or desires? In what ways do you resist love and life?

You are not in your situation to experience it you are there to change it with faith working through love. See the reality of your situation and speak life, love, divine order and health over it. Stir up your desire for more! Then be the architect of your life and create the body and the reality you are here to know… by faith.

5. Train your senses to discern good.

"Taste and see that the Lord is good!" (Psalm 34:8)

Why? Because your body remembers only what it feels or senses, in order to keep your motivation high, positive associations with desired behaviors need to be made.

Every behavior is motivated by the result it produces. According to hedonic theory, you will approach what helps and avoid what hurts. We are all self-regulated by a variety of motives but understanding that pain and pleasure are baselines can bring clarity on cloudy days and get you to the gym when you'd prefer other options.

Choosing life and profit over death and defeat is not natural for most and therefore requires grace to achieve. Not only do you need grace to take action, you need grace to discern your life support team. Right now, in your midst, are resources and people ready to help you achieve your goals. Train your spiritual eyes to recognize them. You will find at least one person, place, or thing equipped and ready to move you in right directions daily, if you are sincerely looking. None of us cross finish lines alone.

Just like the word of God, your desire carries the needed grace to make change. Whether you're training a dog to obedience, a child to wisdom, or an adult to healthy, inspired living, the pleasure pain principle applies. New associations to pleasure are established by disciplining yourself to the new behavior until momentum kicks in and a new kind of pleasure is experienced and associated with the behavior. Before you know it, the old ways become painful and easy to resist. I say resist because there will always be a pull toward living in the flesh, but it loses its power as you exercise authority over it daily.

Change happens when the pain of being a caterpillar outweighs the pain of becoming a butterfly. When you're sick and tired of being sick and tired, 'BAM!' the grace to change arrives.

It's important to see resistance as a thief trying to break in to the house of God (you, His temple), and steal life, love and hope from you. Until you're courageous enough to arise and shine as YOU, he'll find a way in. And until you're willing to give up relationships that are not serving the life and destiny in you, he'll find a way in.

What are the foods, habits, people and places that need to be left behind in order for you to take hold of new and better things? The body you want is yours. It's waiting to be 'claimed.' You will prove your desire for it by acting accordingly in these three areas:

a. Authority. Your ability to keep the thief out of your way and maintain divine order and therefore, proper function continually.
b. Discipline. Your diligence in establishing healthful rituals to keep you on course and running to win.
c. Love. Your ability to express a sincere desire for life, blessing and the perfect will of God.

Closing To Do List:
- Connect daily with compelling reasons you are pursuing change in your body.
- See your new body with your spiritual eyes or imagination.
- Feel the emotions you have in this new body.

- Explore the new tastes, smells and orientations of living in this new body.
- Think and speak in the affirmative concerning your body, "I am healed, strong, well-able, diligent, energized..."
- Through practice, train your thoughts to righteousness, senses to wisdom and body to health.

***

To Contact Stacy:

Stacey Cargnelutti ~ Amore Vita Coaching and Consulting

StaceyC.com ~ Higher Ways & Better Things

Contact me: stacey@staceyc.com

Connect with me: www.facebook.com/StaceyC.com

Mike Greenly & Bill Holmes

Each of us has benefited from decades of experience in meetings and events along with corporate brand-building, strategic marketing and diverse communications assignments. We know what it's like to shoulder sizeable corporate budgets and responsibilities, and to work for companies that produce the motivation that help such clients be successful.

Bill's agency focus expanded in recent years to include industry trade shows, major displays and personalized experiences for attendees. Now back on the client side, he uses internal staff and outside agency talent to help a global healthcare company. You'll find his individual chapter "How I Learned the Value of 'Adjusting" within this book.

Mike, meanwhile, started his corporate career in educational book publishing; then consumer products like toothpaste, margarine and detergent; then direct selling in the beauty business – ultimately becoming the youngest VP (Marketing/Communications) in Avon Products history.

Today he's a freelance speechwriter, script writer, PowerPoint whisperer and executive speech coach. Mike has contributed chapters in CHANGE vol. 8 (how to deliver an effective presentation), vol. 14 (how to write a speech) and vol. 15 (his learnings as a lyricist.) He's had four #1 Billboard-charted Dance Club hits and is the author of the official state anthem of Virginia.

The Power of Paying Attention

By Mike Greenly & Bill Holmes

Foreword (Bill & Mike)

As documented by Wikipedia, on Saturday, August 1, 1981 at 12:01 am, US Eastern Time, MTV launched with these words:

"Ladies and gentleman, rock and roll!"

Those of us around then may remember that the very IDEA of short music videos having their own TV channel, was transformational. More than just a novelty, it actually shifted the culture. Not only did Music TV introduce artists and their new music to young demographics via these dynamic and surprising (back then) videos. MTV was also blamed for reducing human attention spans ... from a half-hour television show, for example, to a three-minute video.

And that was long before the Internet. A Microsoft study in 2015 concluded that human attention spans are now even shorter ... less than the few seconds it takes an average goldfish to focus on any one thing.

But as fast as the pace of life is now, if we learn to take the time to THINK analytically – to NOTICE key signals happening constantly around us – we will be rewarded. The observations we make by "paying attention" can help us be more effective at achieving our goals. There are many examples of the potential benefits of consciously and actively paying attention.

In this chapter, we'll share a few personal experiences and/or learnings about the POWER of paying attention. The two of us – as co-authors in writing it – have collaborated professionally for years on a wide range of meetings and events. We've observed the impact of an effective presentation (content and style) on an audience. We've worked for organizations where a tiny difference in a product or its package design – or the shift of a few words in a TV commercial or sales meeting video – can make a profound difference to one's ultimate success.

Bill has noted the use of such details as the frequent choice of red and yellow for product logos in the fast food industry. Is it a coincidence that both the McDonald's and Burger King logos use those two colors so prominently? Ketchup and mustard, anyone?

Meanwhile, Mike has seen up close the difference it makes in a consumer's perception of a detergent's effectiveness if the color of the inert paint speckles blended into the product are blue ("Wow! This wash looks whiter!") or green ("*Hmmm*! These clothes smell fresher!")

The key is to pay ACTIVE attention in the right way to the right details that are around us all the time. Let's mention some examples ….

Mike

One of the things I love about the work I do in writing speeches and presentations and coaching their effective on-stage delivery is the window I get into different industries and services … continually teaching me as I observe and support my clients up-close.

Among the most interesting things I've learned about … reading about the science and experiencing it in person as part of a DuPont team in the 1980's … is the way that each of us has our own particular styles of thinking. As the DuPont research first taught me, the most successful teams are those that collaborate by recognizing and making the most of each member's DIVERSE approaches to thinking.

There's a model to describe the different ways we each tend to consider things. It's known as "Whole Brain® Thinking", created by physicist, Ned Herrmann. This system pictures our brains as being divided into quadrants ... each one having its own particular emphasis on how we think. (The truth of this concept shows up in MRI's of actual human brain activity.)

How do you, as an individual, tend to make decisions in YOUR life? Are you ANALYTICAL? ... EXPERIMENTAL? ... PRACTICAL? ... RELATIONAL? Each of those traits is visualized as a Quadrant of your brain. The more you approach your life and its decisions in one of those ways, the more a particular brain quadrant affects/describes your personality.

Obviously individual styles and their nuances differ from one person to another. Each of us is different, with varying degrees of dominance among the quadrants of our brains. The resulting balance in our individual selves as we ponder decision "X" helps to define how we approach our lives.

In a Rational way, for example? "Just the facts, ma'am." Or Intuitively? "I'll follow my hunch." How much are we each guided by our intellects – the impact of "facts" on our decisions? Versus acting based on our instincts?

Dr. Herrmann's brain model describes the balance of activity reflected in each of our own brain quadrants with every choice we make. This way of understanding the brain has enabled entire teams and organizations to become more effective ... together. The most successful teams are those that enable its members each to contribute the best of themselves in the styles and ways of thinking that are true to who they are.

It turns out that – big surprise – if you're in sales (or any position where you can benefit by influencing another person's opinion) ... the more astutely you pay attention to the thinking style of the individual you want to influence, the more successful you will tend be.

I made use of Dr. Herrmann's model when I led a Presentation Skills workshop in Lyon, France for my pharma client's sales directors who had come there for an annual conference.

Suppose you're a sales rep, competing for a doctor's time and attention during the precious few minutes you have in his/her office – IF you can get through the door in the first place. How do you make the most of your sales call?

Well, paying attention to the "details" you observe in the room as you shake the doctor's hand can help you tailor your message and style – right on the spot -- in a way that increases your chance of success.

Do you see or feel evidence in the office décor of a strong influence by one of the conceptual brain quadrants? How strongly does your potential customer's way of thinking indicate a style that is Analytical? Experimental? Practical? Or Relational? Simple example: what do you notice on the doctor's walls and on his/her desktop?

If you see a preponderance of *scientific* charts, journals, and data, then use the details you've observed to emphasize the research data behind your medication's effectiveness. On the other hand, if you notice an array of personal photos of spouse, children, pets, etc., this physician might be more inclined to relate to an emphasis on the *experiential* human benefits of the drug you're representing as the solution to a medical problem.

The paragraph above is just one simplistic nugget from the entire presentation. I included role plays in the workshop, as each of sales leaders took a turn in simulating how he/she would shift their current product presentation to underscore different selling points ... based on the details they had spotted and considered in the doctor's office.

The idea of Paying Attention starts with one's own self. I've seen in other people, and have experienced for myself, the value of paying attention to whatever one is instinctively drawn to and is good at. In my case, for example, I truthfully describe myself as a guy who can barely change a light bulb. I'm clueless about what's under the hood of a car and I can injure myself hanging a picture on the wall.

But at least I've learned that Words are my friends, whether I'm writing them or delivering them. Even more so after conquering stage fright and discovering how to make a better and more authentic connection with an audience. I shared some of that knowledge in the chapter I wrote for volume 8 of the CHANGE book series. I draw from my accumulated learnings, of course, every time I coach an executive or team to be more comfortably persuasive on-stage.

Learning to leverage the power of paying attention has helped me with my own life, while giving me the satisfaction of being able to help others – whether writing for them or coaching them. And as Bill is about to show with a personal example of his own, the result of noticing our environment – really paying attention to it – can pay off in satisfying ways.

Bill

Mike mentioned the analysis of human brain quadrants. That study documents the fact that we're all blessed with brains that can think qualitatively and quantitatively. Certainly there's a mechanical aspect to some of our thinking processes, but we are also influenced by emotion -- the visceral impact of the varying experiences and environments we each encounter every day.

It was the human brain in the first place that led to the invention of today's powerful computers. That achievement is a symbol of our potential to harness our intellectual and creative powers in order to see more clearly ... to amplify the truths in front of us ... and to think things through with more wisdom.

We hope this chapter will be a consciousness-raiser for you. That does not mean having to change your whole behavior. It's just being aware that you – each of us – can more actively USE everything we observe, even as we act and do. Because no matter WHAT we do, we are still thinking!

But remember: "hearing" is not the same as "listening." "Seeing" is not the same as truly "observing." The difference comes from CONSCIOUSLY paying attention.

Consider a crime scene, for example. We all have watched and marveled at TV shows over the years – "C.S.I." and others – as we've seen detectives put together the clues that start adding up as they notice "details." Their success comes not just from "collecting" evidence but from actively paying attention to what it means.

Investigators can gather dust, blood, fingerprints, footprints, fibers, hairs and broken glass. All of that may indicate that a crime has taken place, but it's the active processing of this "data" that leads to accurate conclusions.

Learning from our environment is what allows us to adapt to it as we better thrive within it. Paying attention to our surroundings is what enables us to actively adapt, using what we understand to better achieve our goals.

Here is an example I will never forget. When my son Ian was six years old, I introduced him to a world of pleasure that I have loved and appreciated my entire life: Fishing.

I have always loved being outdoors and I greatly enjoy "the world beneath the water." When I was younger, a neighbor introduced me to fly fishing and I was hooked immediately.

Over the years, the generations-old image of a child fishing off the dock with a bobber in the water has morphed into the mindset of fully understanding the science of fishing … and the preparation

The Change[16]

required to maximize success while optimizing both the efficiency and enjoyment of doing it.

Which is what I remembered and re-lived as I enjoyed watching my son fish. I was, and still am, amazed at the exquisite preparation Ian makes, long before he ever puts his line into the water. It would begin the night before our trip: he would check out the weather forecast. He would analyze everything about the day we had planned. Then he would rig his fishing rods based on the kinds of fish we were planning to catch and the conditions we were preparing to face.

The next morning when we arrived at our destination, from the moment we emerged from the car, my son's avid preparation and focus on the details around us would get to a ground level. I remember marveling as I watched him look up at the sky, taking note of wind speed and direction. He would often comment on how the weather conditions – whether cloudy or bright sunshine – would affect where his fish might be on a given day. Some fish feed off the top of the water and other feed in the depths. Some react more to cloudy days and others prefer direct sunlight. His preparations reflected his methodical study.

As we walked to the pond, stream or river, his eyes would gaze out to the water in front of us. Often in the early morning light, as one walks toward water, it is possible to notice the remarkable hatching of insects … as insect pupas on the surface of the water actually hatch simultaneously … taking flight with countless insects all leaving the water and ascending into the air together.

As we started getting closer to the water, Ian would turn over rocks for a serious examination of the ground underneath. Or he would try to catch some of the insects that were flying around near us. Then he would look into his fly box to "match the hatch" with a fly that resembled the native insect of that particular moment of the day …

choosing his lure to look appetizingly like what the trout were searching for at the time.

On a rainy day, for example, insects on the low-hanging branches over the stream would wash into the water in the rainfall. That occurrence of nature would set in place a chain reaction of events that would drastically alter the normal food chain in the stream. It would therefore require the fisherman's ability to adapt to it rapidly and accurately. This new abundance of food gave Ian fresh clues from a different perspective, shedding light on how to match his hunt to the details of that moment. Long before he put his line into the water, Ian had learned 10 things that would influence his behavior and increase his chances of success that day.

I was astonished at my son's intensity -- how he would go "an inch wide and a mile deep" in his devotion to the activity. Other boys his age would have comic books all over the floor of their room, but Ian's room was strewn with books, journals and magazines – all about fishing! This was a genuine passion for him. I remember trudging all over Lake Placid, NY, just to get the autograph of an 88-year-old fly fisherman who had written Ian's favorite book.

My son thrived on paying close attention to the world around him in order to build his knowledge for any given moment … and then put his observations into practice. Mind you, not every day was successful. But he understood that his careful preparation – first paying attention and then using what he took in – would optimize his chances of catching whatever he was after.

I can still envision one particular day in Vermont. We were fishing at a small pond and Ian spotted a large bass lying in the reeds. He studied the condition of the pond and started experimenting with different colored lures and plastic worms … placing each one gently onto the water, time after time. He'd adjust to what he experienced -- changing the colors he used and casting into different spots until he found the right combination. Then … WHAM! The bass went for the bait and was hooked! Even just seeing that kind of excitement and accomplishment in a young child is incredibly inspiring.

Reading and studying your environment to know what went into the commission of a crime, the successful catching of fish or achieving whatever goal you're after ... has parallels in our business and personal lives. Paying attention helps you anticipate what people are looking for and expecting in their interactions with you. There's a reason the old saying has lasted so long: "Knowledge IS power."

CLOSING (Bill & Mike)

Perhaps our message seems a bit "basic" to you. Well it is, actually ... but we would also suggest that it's more relevant and needed than ever.

America and the world as a whole continue to become more digital and mobile at once. This statement goes beyond what you'll see on any urban street: the number of people walking straight ahead, while directing their gazes down to the phones clutched their hands.

In fact, some 2016 research from www.eMarketer.com showed that the younger the generation of consumers who were surveyed, the more fervently they avoid looking up from their phones as they lead their lives, including making purchases. Only 28% of seniors (ages 69+) stated a preference for shopping digitally versus in-store. For consumers ages 18-34, however, over two thirds (67%) PREFER to purchase online. The array of Apps for mobile phones continues to increase this habit.

But ... a few questions. As our faces are buried in a downward stare toward our phones, what details are we missing around us?

And if our attention spans have become historically shortened as we've gotten used to virtually "instant" results from Google, etc., what details are we missing in the world around us? From making a sales call to trying to catch a fish ... from the detective solving a crime … to the driver in a car … to the pedestrian just crossing the street … what details are we missing that could actually enrich our lives and pursuits?

The only way to DISCOVER the power of paying attention is to allow yourself to do so! The two of us are better off by having added that consciousness to our lives.

Bill & Mike

Mike Greenly:

greenlypro@mikegreenly.com

Bill Holmes:

wjholmes5@gmail.com

office land line: 212-758-5338

mobile: 917-447-5211

mobile: 646-247-7936

Erin McDonnell

Erin McDonnell is considered by all who know her – family, friends, colleagues and the people she helps in her daily work – as a smart, caring, conscientious person. Early on in life, she seems to have intuited that her mission would be to help others in a career focused on Human Services.

After receiving her B.S. in Human Services at Fisher College in Boston, she put her skills to work as a Social Worker Technician for the Department of Children and Families Harbor Area Office in Chelsea, MA.

From there, she provided support and encouragement at the New Chardon Street Homeless Shelter for Women and Children in Boston ... became a Community Resource Specialist for Work Inc. in Dorchester, MA. ... a Human Services worker, intern and volunteer at Women's Lunch Place in Boston ... now serving as Social Worker with the Mass. Department of Children and Families in Boston.

Given the person Erin is, no one in her life was surprised when she decided to write this CHANGE chapter about her struggles with eating disorders and depression. Her greatest hope is that it will be helpful to people who share this struggle and to everyone who loves them.

Overcoming Eating Disorders & Depression

By Erin McDonnell

Do you know anyone with an eating disorder? Even if not a victim, yourself, chances are you know at least someone hiding her/his condition in plain sight. I know about the topic first-hand, having suffered from it for years.

The National Institute of Mental Health (NIMH) defines eating disorders as a set of "serious and sometimes fatal illnesses that cause severe disturbances to a person's eating behaviors." These problems can affect all ages, but tend to be at least twice as prevalent among females.

For all of us, though, food is connected to emotion in our culture. Even soft drinks can be advertised with a halo message: "Drink me and your life will be more joyful!" From potato chips to hamburgers to pizza, food is often presented as a doorway into happiness … versus the imprisonment that food addiction actually can create.

I used to be too ashamed to reveal my battle with addiction. Today, though, I am stronger – having left my shame behind.

That strength is what I hope to share this chapter. I'd like to be of help to others still suffering as I was. I'd also like to be supportive and informative if *you* love and care about someone else still in the grip of this sickness. And that, indeed, is what eating disorders are: *sickness!*

So let me pose a question about your everyday life ….

When you walk into a supermarket, what do you see? Employees at the front, scanning products into their cash registers? Flyers promoting "specials" and discounts? A selection of shopping carts and baskets?

Here's what I used to experience when I stepped inside a supermarket: *myself* on the verge of losing all control.

I knew each time that there was a heightened chance I was about to have a panic attack. I was *obsessed* with food and I'd just entered its headquarters! My eyes would dart from one product to the next, on as many shelves as I could see, trying to take them all in.

Yes: I was the annoying person taking up time and space in the aisles while studying the nutrition content of every box, jar or can. I was the one standing in your way, taking so long to make the earth-shaking decision of ... whether or not to eat a banana.

Being a functioning anorexic and bulimic means that each thought is plagued with the time- and energy-sucking obstacle of irrational thinking. The food and health consciousness that first became my way to lose weight, later became a full-fledged *obsession* with becoming the skinniest version of "me" I could ... all in my attempt to garner love and respect, as though only food could help me attain that prize.

Does your body's fat content determine your worth? Of course not! But for the last decade or so, I actually believed that it did for *me*.

Succumbing to the desire to eat a piece of fruit felt, to me, like abject failure. Each time I gave into the temptation of eating a few raw almonds, I wanted to punish myself for losing the war inside my head.

I'm over that now – Hooray! But let me take you back to the start of my journey, to shed some light on what living with an eating disorder can do to one's mind, body and life.

I've never had an issue making friends. In high school, I was surrounded by a close knit group of girlfriends. I lived a fulfilling life.

I was about 40-50 pounds heavier than I am now, but I wasn't born believing I was unworthy. That I learned over time.

Back then, I felt no discomfort with how I looked. I was heavily involved in extracurricular activities, including city basketball and soccer leagues on weekends. I spent happy times with friends, enjoying the freedom of being teenager with little responsibility.

As time progressed and my confidence grew, I began sensing strong waves of distaste from others. I'd been raised to be respectful and responsible -- honoring my commitments to my friendships and my studies. But it seemed that the happier (and heavier) I became, the more upset others became about me.

The "message" was clear: I did *not* deserve to like or enjoy myself, given the weight and size of my body.

Bullying is a cruel reality that everyone endures at some point. During my high school senior year, as I began actually dating, I discovered that some boys whose requests I politely declined, came back with harsh retorts directed at my weight and putting me down.

Any form of bullying is disgraceful, but this was insidious: making me wonder if I even *deserved* to be happy, given that I was considered "fat."

One memory stands out in particular. I was close friends with someone in high school whom I heard had called me a "fat whore" behind my back. I was devastated!

I remember getting the news after eating pasta for lunch. The first thing I did – even before letting myself cry -- was run into the bathroom to stick my fingers down my throat. Vomit covered my hands and tears streamed down my face. I promised myself that I'd do everything I could to lose weight and become desirable to men.

What breaks my heart as I look back on that day was my total inability to think that I was a worthy person already. I'd let someone else determine my worth, simply by judging my weight.

But I kept the promise to myself and began a new way of life. After every lunch, I'd secretly stick my fingers down my throat to release everything I'd eaten. I'd wait for people to leave the neighboring stalls before purging even more, in order to keep my problem private.

Fast forward through the summer after graduation: I moved to Boston for college. I did my best to maintain a healthy regimen and lose weight in ways that wouldn't damage my body. I joined a gym, ate more wisely and managed to lose 20 pounds.

I felt comfortable with my progress during one of the best years of my life. My purging seemed far behind me.

The following year, I began dating. I'd met someone who intrigued me and we formed a relationship. I was proud to be with a smart, successful, and educated man. The only problem? He reminded me constantly that I represented none of those traits.

More importantly, I now look back and remember that, in the beginning of our relationship, he'd make comments about a stranger's weight and about my eating habits. That should have been a red flag! But I was so excited to be with someone of his caliber, that I readily sacrificed my own ideals ... like openly speaking my mind.

Instead, I quietly allowed myself to be bullied in order to keep hearing him say he loved me. I felt caught between two worlds – love and shame – in one relationship ... constantly feeling the whiplash between one emotion and the other.

On the one hand, he made me laugh ... supporting me as best he could and trying to understand me. On the other hand, he wanted a life I wasn't ready for. And a body I didn't offer.

I was slowly losing my identity, trying to become the person *he* wanted so I could stay in a relationship I felt lucky to have. But over time, I began to resent what felt like his oppression – not actual acceptance or love.

The Change[16]

I'd surrendered myself to "The Relationship" … no longer spending much time on my own interests or with my friends. It was great feeling loved (even with implicit "expectations" for my needed weight loss) but my family felt that I'd subdued myself and had lost my own voice.

One day I made the decision to end things. I felt horribly guilty for hurting someone I'd spent years planning a life with, but I also felt liberated from trying to be someone else in order to please him.

And … I was confused.

I poured myself into work, school, meaningless sex and spending time with friends. But none of that aided my quest to rediscover myself. So I began to re-visit an old pattern: my eating disorder, which felt like the only way to rediscover myself.

I began to lose weight quickly. I went to the gym two hours a day and ate only salads with no dressing or protein. I began skipping dinner, just drinking coffee to suppress my hunger.

I felt invincible: I didn't need food to function! My hunger pangs felt like signals that I was doing something right. I lacked control over anything else, but I'd regained control over my body and that focus became my life.

After losing 40 pounds, I heard disparagement turn to compliments. Everyone said how great I looked. It seemed I'd finally accomplished something meaningful: being thin was my ticket to happiness and success!

But while the praise was sweet to hear, it also became an excuse for me to further indulge in my eating disorder. I began eating only one meal a day – lunch – after which, I'd hurry into the nearest bathroom and stick my fingers down my throat.

I was ashamed of doing it. But each time, after the food had been purged, I felt euphoria! I had discovered the power to *make* myself thin … my own secret weapon.

I was now obsessed with maintaining my lowest possible weight. I weighed myself twice a day and kept journals noting which foods were easiest to purge. I visited pro-anorexia websites to learn how to be even thinner!

I was lying to my friends to explain why I wouldn't join them to eat, claiming that I was "sick" or too busy with "work." My #1 fixation was the need to be "thin." I was constantly exhausted, forcing myself to work out with no food in my body ... only to end up feeling dizzy and passing out on the gym bathroom floor.

Whatever money I'd normally spend on food was now devoted to zero calorie drinks to help fill my stomach and banish my hunger cues. The only reasons I'd leave home were for work or the gym. And here's how irrational food disorders can be: I looked the thinnest I'd ever been yet felt embarrassed not to be even smaller!

Next came paranoia. Every time I left the house, I felt people were staring at me, mocking me for my weight. I used that fear as motivation at the gym to push myself even harder.

My family began worrying as they saw less and less of me, literally and figuratively. I would trap myself in my apartment and cry daily: I didn't know what else to do. I was my own prisoner, locking myself in my bedroom for being unattractive. I had the keys to "get out of jail" but wouldn't use them for myself. I felt helpless.

One day I noticed a rash on my legs -- spider veins of some sort. I ignored my own condition, assuming it was just temporary. But the rash seemed to get worse, and my concern grew

Finally, after visiting various hospitals and clinics and several doctors who were mystified ... and even after a biopsy of my leg ... one doctor asked the question to obtain the answer I'd been too ashamed to divulge: "Is there anything else that might be helpful to tell me?" asked?

(Gulp!)

"Yes," I said. "I have an eating disorder."

Immediately he knew what was wrong: "levido reticulis" on my legs. It's caused by a lack of nutrients and creates blood clots that form a rash, which looks just like spider veins. I'd done this to myself: my refusal to eat had created the rash.

I was both relieved and ashamed to learn what had caused my problem. But even this news wasn't enough to help me refrain from restricting and purging my meals. I held on to the disorder for dear life.

Eventually, loneliness caught up with me and I sank even deeper into depression. I wasn't comfortable acknowledging that I had a problem, but the more obvious it got, the more the people around me urged me to get help. I thanked them and assured them: I'd fix it on my own.

One weekend, I went skiing with my family and had a wonderful time. On the ride home with my brother and sister-in-law, we stopped at a Dunkin' Donuts for breakfast. I ate a bagel with cream cheese and felt incredibly satisfied. I was present emotionally, engaging in conversation instead of disassociating and thinking about food. This was one of the few moments at the time when I was genuinely happy.

After getting back home, I body checked, lifting my shirt to discover that my stomach was bloated. I was horrified and swore never to eat another bagel again. I called my friend and cried hysterically. She cried, too. "Please, get help. You're scaring me." I felt like I'd hit rock bottom.

I had plans the next day with my brother but I lacked the courage to leave the apartment. He pleaded with me to meet him and even offered to come to me, but I wouldn't allow anyone to see me in this state. I know he was scared just hearing me.

I called my Mom an hour later and said, "I think something's wrong. I have a problem and I need help."

She helped right away!

Up until that moment, I'd kept myself in isolation, countless therapy sessions, fainting in public, dizzy spells daily and lonely nights in my apartment ... even the blood red and dark brown rashes on my legs: none of that was enough to encourage me to seek more substantial help.

I guess everyone has their moments of crisis in life. Mine was staring at myself in the mirror, with dry brittle skin, my cheeks stained with the aftermath of my tears ... all alone in my apartment and feeling helpless.

With my mother's help, I entered inpatient treatment at an eating disorder clinic in Boston. I was terrified, but ready to make a change from being broken, depressed, ashamed and lonely. I reluctantly walked through the doors of the clinic ... and altered my life.

It was the hardest month I'd ever endured. The staff watched me eat each meal. The other patients and I openly discussed the emotions we were numbing with our eating disorder behaviors – insecurity, fear, depression and so on.

It was hard enough that I'd had to ask for a medical leave from work, but now to be in a program and fully facing my disorder head on: the experience was horrifying! Every bite of food I took made me want to burst into tears, but watching other powerful women around me fighting their fears, too, while also feeling their vulnerability – well, that support was immensely helpful to my recovery.

I gained some incredible friends from the treatment. It altered my life completely. Even as I said goodbye to the frighteningly skinny girl who'd arrived at the clinic ... I regained my own real self.

Letting go of trying to control everything – including my fixation on every calorie -- helped me find ultimate freedom from my disorder.

I'd thought I been in an unhealthy relationship with a man, but the truth is: my anorexia and bulimia was the *most* unhealthy relationship I'd ever had.

My recovery is now on-going, just as is true with recovering alcoholics. It will always be a struggle to combat my disordered thoughts.

And while my relationship with my food and body image has vastly improved, I still have days where I want to isolate myself and blindly restrict nourishment from my body. But with the effective tools I learned from therapy, I've created much healthier ways of coping with my anxiety and depression. Food restriction became my own form of self-harm while giving me a false sense of confidence.

Today, I am stronger because I am not ashamed of my past. I'm no longer afraid to walk into a grocery store. I no longer fear an anxiety attack over nutrition labels. And I no longer feel the need to numb my emotions by restricting my food and depriving myself of human connections.

Learning to be open and vulnerable has been one of the most empowering feelings I've ever had. At times I look back and want to cry, because it hurts me to remember that so many men and women in the world are still struggling with eating disorders … without the resources, support or insurance to get help and improve their lives. I realize how lucky I was, to have had a support system at home and around me that encouraged me each step of the way, despite my occasional resistance.

If I could leave you with one take-away I've gained from all this, it's not to be afraid of your problems. As terrifying as it can be, I've learned that the best way to conquer hardships, is to have the courage to be vulnerable and face them head on.

So speak up when you're struggling! *Accept* the help that others offer you. Reaching out for support is not a sign of weakness but of strength and resilience. We can each get so distracted by our quests to become the best possible versions of ourselves, that we forget to give ourselves credit for any progress we've actually made.

This I can promise: you're not alone in your pursuit of happiness.

Expose yourself to others as I finally learned to do. You'll connect with them on a deeper level than you ever thought possible. And that will make all the difference!

***

To contact Erin:

email: Erinmcdonnell903@gmail.com

mobile: 617-816-5244

Jimmy Star

Jimmy Star is the host of The Jimmy Star Show with Ron Russell, the #1 Webshow (radio/television) in the world with 4.5 million weekly viewers/listeners.

He is an award-winning publicist in the Entertainment Industry, and was named the fifth most influential person in radio to follow in social media. Jimmy Star is ranked in top half of one percent of all 1.8 billion social media users in the world.

Secrets of Social Media Success

By Jimmy Star

These days, most brands, celebrities, businesses, creatives, musicians, artists, authors, filmmakers -- and the fans of all of these pursuits -- use social media in one form or another. Unfortunately, though, many extremely talented groups and individuals don't yet fully understand how to harness the POWER of social media, using it to their advantage by maximizing its potential as a highly useful tool for networking effectively with others.

Let me emphasize the point. If you really want to be successful with social media, it's crucial to understand that success comes from much more than merely tossing up a post or two a day – as though that were enough to achieve your social media "homework" for the day. NO! To have real social media success, you need to actively and socially network, not blast commercials at people as though you were a living billboard.

The Only Cost: Your Time and Focus. Social media is a no-cost marketing medium that offers huge reach and impact. The only "cost" is your time and attention. Your success rate is directly related to the amount of time and focus you devote to using and promoting as an active user of it.

Social media gives today's user the ability to reach out and connect to thousands of fans, customers, contemporaries and potential business associates. But real social media SUCCESS requires a serious investment of your time. So … if you want to achieve real results, you need to formulate a plan of attack for YOUR social media marketing efforts. Also, be sure that whatever you do personally is integrated with any other marketing and advertising programs being used for your brand or business.

It's a Conversation, Not a Marketing Bulletin. Think of social media as having a conversation with a friend. When you meet or chat with your friends, you're NOT giving them a marketing speech! You're just having fun sharing and talking with them. Networking should be based on meaningful conversations where the social media aspect adds an intrinsic value, WITHOUT being an Infomercial.

Make sure you are talking WITH your audience and not TO them. You want to engage your audience, not "preach" at them. Without engagement, you're simply talking at people. You might as well be a machine. And that's exactly how consumers will view you! Once you're perceived to be (or to be like) a machine or a bot, it's hard to change that perception. So be sure you're engaging people socially from the very start of your social media adventure.

Be "Social!" The biggest limiter I see to social media success is not being "social." It's called Social Media for a reason, so use the media to BE that: social! It doesn't matter which platform you're using -- Twitter, Facebook, Instagram, Pinterest, YouTube, LinkedIn, Google+, Snapchat or any others of the media that pop up on a daily basis. It is VERY important to reciprocate and respond to everyone who engages with you. Be sure to listen to others who are engaging with you, and respond appropriately.

Reality: this takes time! I can hear the sighs of exhaustion already, but no one said this would be easy. Social media influencers have accrued opportunities that the rest of the world would love to have, too. But attaining that level of impact doesn't happen overnight. You have to WORK to see results.

Learn to budget your time and make it fun. Meeting new people with the same interests as your own should be a fun way to network and promote yourself and your business in a friendly fashion. Be sure to follow and engage with individuals and businesses that are in the same fields as yourself.

You may not want to become an international social media influencer. Maybe you just want be great at networking to make friends and build clients for your products and services. That's what social media was set up to do.

Interaction is one of the hallmarks of social media. Indeed, interaction is why social media is such a valuable tool for marketing in the first place. Talking "with" your customers is the first step in getting them to talk "about" you and your company. That's what you want: to generate conversations and attention. People love it when a business responds directly to them, and social media makes doing so easier than ever. You just need to dedicate the time and resources to do it. That's the REALITY.

Share Content with Others. Along with being social, it's important to share content to become successful in the social media arena. Sharing fuels growth.

When you share interesting content that came from someone else, you're giving a great compliment to the originator of the material you passed along to others. It is VERY important to do that with content you find of genuine interest and value.

When you share content from someone else, they in turn will share yours. That's how you grow your social media network. As your network grows, so will your influence, which in turn will increase the productivity of your network.

The bigger your network becomes, the larger your audience will be … which (it's a positive cycle!) further increases your potential to network and sell your product or service.

"The 80/20 Rule." This rule is what Wikipedia reminds us is the Pareto principle. A limited amount of the right action can lead to a widespread result.

Apply this to your social media strategy: use 20% of your content to promote yourself, brand or company. But dedicate 80% of your focus to content that genuinely interests you and your audience ... news, entertainment, whatever topics interest YOU – making observations and sharing content that will engage your followers in conversation.

Social media is about building RELATIONSHIPS. "The 80/20 Rule" will help you do that instead of upsetting and annoying your audience with content that's irrelevant to others and merely boosts your narcissistic ego and image. Compile the 80% content from influencers whose ideas you like and agree with, and which cater to the interests and needs of your audience. Once you find appropriately engaging content, share it on your social media channels.

Be original. Try to think outside the box, posting your own original content while also sharing content from others. Use your posts to seek engagement. Test different ideas to see which kinds of posts your audience responds to. Be sure to avoid delivering the same message over and over.

Interact. Measure your engagement not just in the numbers of followers you attract. It's also important to FOLLOW OTHERS ... accounts and people that are part of your target audience or industry. When following these accounts, engage with them. Leave comments, ask questions or tag them in posts that you think are relevant to the two you.

Once you begin interacting this way, you'll be able to create a relationship. The accounts with which you show a genuine interest are more likely to engage back with you and with the content you put out to the world. These interactions will increase your organic (unpaid) reach.

Be human! This tip about achieving social media success may throw you for a loop. But I'm serious: it's crucial to remember to let yourself be HUMAN in your quest for success in this modern way of relating.

When parameters are similar or the same -- and in the competitive world we live in today, things almost always are -- people are more interested in learning who YOU are, personally, as a human being. It also helps to have them learn about the PEOPLE who make up your team. Others may have similar ideas or services, but you and your team are uniquely YOU.

As people become comfortable with who you are, they'll more naturally choose to support the products or services you offer. So you want to SHOW who you are in your social media interactions.

The people we admire – those who give us our most important life lessons as role models – become important to us. Only rarely do we feel the same emotional engagement with a brand. So strive to have you and your team inspire and motivate your community based on the people you actually ARE … and as the team you comprise together.

Always treat your customers, prospects and advocates like human beings whose opinions actually matter to you. Which they should!

Be genuine. Always be who you are. That will help you stand out and attract your audience as you go along. Share the good and bad times with your followers and friends. No person or organization is just roses, lollipops and balloons every day.

Let your social media reflect the good AND bad, the ugly AND beautiful that come with your successes and struggles. Show your humility and be authentic. That will do wonders for your social media success. Individuals and businesses that are genuine and real are the ones that people most trust, follow, engage and interact with The result can be a customer base of loyal users for your products and services.

Put a face to your brand or company. Everyone – whether an individual, company or brand – has a "face" that people can identify with … if it feels REAL.

Remember to Interact! Pay attention to all the comments you receive, and make sure you reply to all of them. Social media is meant to let people know who you are on a personal level, going beyond what you'd find on a typical website. It's super important not to drop the ball and ignore comments. If you fail to reply or acknowledge, people will notice and head over to someone else who's more responsive to them and their comments.

Social media interaction can be different for everyone. Be sure to take note of the times and days when you get the most engagement for you and your business. Post your content when your traffic is the busiest and where you experience a greater progression of growth or engagement. Knowing the best times to connect with your specific audience will help you stand out and not get lost in all the commotion on social media.

Track your success. Track your social media success. Measure your program and be sure that it's worth your investment of the time you're devoting to it. Most social media platforms offer analytic tools to monitor the user's progress. If you can't find them, just take a look at the Help section of the platform. You can also measure engagement by the number of comments, likes and connections you receive from your efforts.

Importance of an Image. Be sure to include visuals in your social media campaigns. The majority of social media users prefer to view an image, which takes a minimal amount of time to comprehend. Images tend to engage people more than text.

Remember the saying, "A Picture is Worth a Thousand Words." Research shows that social media photos generate more engagement than posts that do not have any visual elements. Get Creative. Post pictures of you in your everyday life to all your social media accounts. Colorful, eye-catching photos are a great way to maintain current followers while attracting new ones to your social media accounts.

This thought takes me back to the importance of being human and genuine. It is very important to be personal ... real ... authentic. People can see that in your photos if you allow yourself to show it.

Consistently Promote! Steadily make people aware of all of your social media platforms by promoting through your website, brochures, fliers, business cards and any other vehicle you use to increase awareness of you, your brand, your company, your special interest and so on.

Consistency is key. Publish your content on a regular schedule. People will respond more positively to your social media, engage with you more, and more readily subscribe to your updates when they know that you are publishing content they can count on.

You'll see! They'll begin to rely on you to release content and will look forward to frequent new content that they can consume on a regular basis. But don't "force it." It's imperative that you play the long-term game of being patient as you build your social media following. There's no "magic" involved ... just tenacity, humanity and authenticity. Select the media and audiences that are best for what YOU do, and stick with them for a successful social media strategy.

Be Open to Change. Last but not least, I meant that advice above: "stick with" the media and audiences that are best for what you do.

And yet ... remain open to thoughtful change – especially as you first start to consciously define yourself on social media, and as you discover who your brand or your business naturally attracts. You might not develop your best social media marketing campaign on your very first try. It takes time to build a network of people who follow you and share your content.

So while it's certainly important to be patient, if you know you're doing everything you can but you're still not seeing movement of your results in the right direction, it may be time to re-evaluate your content so you can test and explore a new direction. Adjusting your social media strategy as you learn what works and what doesn't for you, your brand or your business is fine as you determine what's best. But again, remember to be CONSISTENT once you've developed a strategy that's really working.

Also keep in mind that social media is evolving by the day. Pay attention to the shifts around us to take full advantage of everything social media has to offer. Never be afraid to make tweaks to what you are doing – even as you maintain your overall strategy -- in order to refine your ability to get the results you seek.

A Personal Word

I'm grateful to have learned the principles of achieving social media success, and I'm honored for the chance to have shared them with you.

It's not just about the "numbers." Being really active has allowed me to build some incredible life-long friendships, along with important business relationships that have propelled my career forward immensely.

Anything I've achieved … from transforming a small radio broadcast -- "The Jimmy Star Show with Ron Russell" – into the #1 Web Television/Radio show in the world … to the awards and honors I've been fortunate to have received … to becoming a successful author and to getting cast in over 40 movies … ALL of that has been directly influenced by my networking through social media.

I get tremendous satisfaction from this passion of mine. If anything I've shared will help YOU get find more pleasure and success from social media, I'm DELIGHTED. Thanks for reading!

***

To Contact Jimmy:

#1 Webshow in World

www.JimmyStarsWorld.com

Now on ROKU Television, Comcast on Demand & iHeart Radio

Follow Jimmy in social media.

Twitter @DrJimmyStar

Instagram @DrJimmyStar

Facebook http://www.facebook.com/jimmystar

Email: JimmyStar@JimmyStarShow.com

Jeff Metz

Jeff Metz serves as President & CEO of Metz Culinary Management. He 30 years of diverse experience in the restaurant business and extensive employee relations management, operational excellence, communications skills and outstanding client partnership.

Today, he oversees more than 300 contract management accounts in 22 states, including the Metz Environmental Services division. He's earned numerous awards for his leadership and his businesses. Jeff was honored, for example, as a 2017 Silver Plate Award recipient by the International Foodservice Manufacturers Association (IFMA), which recognizes excellence in eight segments of foodservice operations.

Beyond his business success, Jeff lives life with an ongoing commitment to the communities around him and his businesses. Among the organizations where he's worked to make a difference are Share Our Strength/No Kids Hungry, the United Way, the Commission on Economic Opportunity (CEO) and the Make-A-Wish Foundation.

He's a Past Chair of the Board of the Pennsylvania Restaurant Association and has served as Chairman of their Political Action and Political Education committees. He is a member of the Young President's Organization and the Penn State SHM Industry Advisory Council. He resides in northeastern Pennsylvania with his wife, Susan, their daughters, Kaitlyn and Ashley and their son, Jeffrey.

People First – Always!

By Jeff Metz

I'm fortunate to head a thriving organization, Metz Culinary Management. It's filled with remarkable people widely considered to represent a standard of quality that helps set us at Metz apart.

BUT ... here's the thing. The "secret sauce" that contributes to our success hasn't come from some advanced research laboratory. Nor from the hallowed halls of The Wharton School of Business or any other fine source of learning.

Instead, the culture and values that are most responsible for our continuing growth and progress have come directly from a very simple source: my father, John Metz. And although we are still a family-owned business, I've become convinced as we've grown (and we're still growing!) that the values that help us succeed would be just as useful for even a multi-BILLION-dollar corporation.

The essence of those values – and the difference they help us achieve each day – is simple and clear: **We always put people FIRST**. Before profits, logistics, or anything else we're involved with. We need to know that we're making a positive difference for people ... our customers, partners and guests. First and foremost, though, we begin with our own employees. What is best for THEM that we are able to achieve?

I think you'll see, as I share our story, that we take our mantra seriously. We LIVE it for real in many diverse ways, big and small.

It all began with my Dad ... and who he naturally is.

My father, John Metz, began his career quite humbly. His father was a truck driver. And his first job was simply ... washing dishes. Even dishwashing is part of "the Hospitality business" and believe me, some of the work is basic. But important!

Soon it will be about 30 years since I got into this business ... first at Heinz, selling ketchup and soups. Eventually I became a TGI Friday's restaurant manager, and I discovered about myself that I really do love our business.

It's just a truth about me: I love hospitality ... serving people with food, doing so with a nice presentation and always with a positive and respectful attitude that helps to make recipients happy. To my mind, hospitality done right always makes people feel individually appreciated and cared for. Ideally, it even helps them be healthy!

In fact, what I have learned is how satisfying it is to share that passion for hospitality and service with others in ANY business who also appreciate making a difference for people and the institutions that support them.

We start by serving our own people!

But here's where my father's influence is so special. Our primary purpose is always to serve others ... and not just our guests. That means serving our fellow team members, too!

As Cheryl McCann (our VP of human resources) always says,

"Our Guest experience can never exceed our Team Member experience."

I believe we live this attitude, first and foremost, because of the modest beginnings and personality of my father, our founder. But I'm convinced that point of view– if practiced sincerely – would make a difference in even the largest corporations on earth.

Actually, several of my friends have been or still are high-ranking Fortune 500 execs. I've been struck by their positive comments as they've learned about how we operate and the way that we treat our people.

One VP wishes his own large company could treat its people as we do. All I can tell you is: it works! Maybe one day, my friend will

The Change[16]

inspire his corporation to look in a mirror and see if they might want to start treating their own folks with more consideration. As I believe you'll see from this chapter, such genuine concern is motivating to those who receive it.

I'll offer you a few illustrations very shortly. But you'll better understand their impact on people if I first share more of a context: exactly who WE are.

Metz Culinary Management: Not "Institutional!"

You know, already, that we're a "family" organization – a regionally-based food service company that my father founded in 1994. Food service means that we handle the meals for a broad range of organizations and institutions. We also have an environmental services division where we handle maintenance, house cleaning, transportation, etc. In addition, we own and operate a number of restaurants including Ruth's Chris Steakhouse, TGI Fridays, Wolfgang Puck and Chick-fil-A.

Just think of the different groups of constituents in the world who get their food from a central cafeteria – that's who we feed! Our approach is different. We don't even call them "cafeterias." They're dining halls and cafés to us. It's a different aspiration. Colleges and universities, hospitals and senior care facilities, independent schools, public K-12, corporations and so on.

Every audience – each "segment of the market" to use the business analytic term – has its own special needs and circumstances. But guess what? All of them are PEOPLE!

I'll bet you've experienced at some point in your life – at some "institution" where you were dining – the almost robotic process of grabbing a tray and silverware … and then step by step – in sequence, like a chain gang – navigating around the bins of various food choices. Often these dishes were prepared quite a while before you stepped into the process. By the time you get there, they may or may not be the freshest possible selection.

Well, early on in our history, we determined to differentiate ourselves ... by offering food with a "restaurant style" mindset and a focus on "hospitality." There's no mystery about the word's meaning: "the friendly and generous reception and entertainment of guests, visitors, or strangers."

The only "mystery" is why that spirit is not more widely experienced in so many of the group dining settings that are a part of so many of our lives.

After all, in many locations we service, the diners have CHOICES. They don't have to eat with us. Maybe they can order meals from "a real restaurant" using delivery services with names like Seamless, Uber Eats, Grubhub, DoorDash, Postmates, etc.

So SERVING our meals in "institutions" doesn't mean our food needs to TASTE "institutional" ... or that it feels impersonal, as in: "Next in line? Keep it movin'!"

Having dinner with family or friends feels different than dining with strangers. At Metz we work to bring a personal, family feel to our service WHEREVER we happen to be.

Even food in institutions can feel and be more "personal." But that's a spirit that starts with the people at each site who represent the servicing company. How can those servers and other staff channel a personal experience of respect, warmth and nature for others if they don't experience it, themselves, from the organization they're a part of.

We reflect a spirit of caring about others even in simple ways like the "labels" we use to refer to others. So we call our clients our "partners" – as a built-in reminder, every time we use the word, of the SPIRIT we want to reflect. And their diners aren't their "customers" to us – they're "Guests."

And regardless of the fact that my title is President and CEO ... that my father is Executive Chairman ... that my sister, Maureen, is VP

Marketing and Purchasing … or that my brother, John Jr., is President of his own foodservice company, Sterling Spoon … you can easily find any of us, happily pitching in on-site to help a guest have a better, more satisfying and more delicious experience.

"Restaurant Style" Hospitality

So picture being a patient in a hospital – which almost all of us have visited, if not actually been patients ourselves. You're NOT just "a patient." As far as we're concerned, you're also a "guest" and deserve to be treated as such. Just as if you were staying at a Four Seasons Hotel, you can phone down for Room Service. We'll bring your own personal selections right to your bed.

Or you can have what we call "Spoken" service. Don't want to bother to read? Not feeling up to it? We'll send a host or hostess directly up to you room … and he or she will personally READ you the choices of the day. Take your order, come back with your food, come back again to be sure you're happy!

I was describing this service to a friend the other day and he said, "Wait! What? This is in a HOSPITAL, right? That kind of personal service actually IN a hospital?"

Yes! And that's the point: treating people like PEOPLE.

Back to that tray-carrying "chain gang" I was describing earlier, where you shuffle around a long table – rotating past choices that don't appeal to you as you look for what actually does.

Well, now – with us, at least – your dining feels more like you're in an open and celebrative food hall. Food choices are set into separately located hubs, so you can go straight to your heart's (or stomach's) desire.

Go to Main Plate for Entrees. Go to the Grill for a freshly made burger or chicken sandwich. Visit the Pizza station for pizza or pasta. Go to the deli for a sandwich that is freshly custom-made for YOU.

By the way – unlike many of the fast food outlets, we never freeze our burgers. We make fresh patties for our diners from freshly ground beef.

It's a "mentality" – treating our guests (and our partners' guests) like a beloved part of the family. Our job when we're serving our partners' guess is to make them feel that they're OUR guests, too. We want to know, feel and taste that our service is personal and aiming to please – not a function we're "implementing" like robots in a factory to assemble a car.

How People Act in a "People First" Culture

It's as basic as the Golden Rule – treating others as we, ourselves, would wish to be treated. But doesn't it just make simple common sense? The more respected and well-treated our employees are, the more they'll know what it FEELS like to treat clients and guests the same way.

Let me share some examples I'm proud of … proud of our people who made them happen because they WANTED to!

Example: We learned one of our associates in healthcare was illiterate.

His General Manager challenged the team to create visuals with the correctly spelled definition to help him identify letters and form words. So a hand-drawn picture of a pot had the word "POT" spelled right beside the illustration.

That GM took two more steps to support and continue the process. First he borrowed reading and word-identification books from his church and then shared his mission for the employee. Having discovered the goal, we contributed $1,000 from Metz to help the employee's dream of literacy come true. Today he can read! And, believe me, he knows what caring about others feels like.

More examples:

Remember the Pulse nightclub shooting in Orlando in June of 2016? Metz worked with Barry University's Dwayne O. Andreas School of Law to provide food and water to hundreds of first responders who helped with that terrible need.

Our volunteers prepared and delivered dinner for 125 people at the Emergency Operations Center ... cooked a hot meal for 35 employees at the Red Cross headquarters ... and supplied breakfast for two days at the Medical Examiner's office.

Metz Culinary Management has gladly assisted in the preparation of meals and services for several hurricanes over the past few years, including Matthew and Irma.

In addition, our team at Maryville College in Knoxville, TN assisted with the collection of donations and supplies in response to wildfires there in 2016.

My father's been this way all along

I was about three years old when Hurricane Agnes created a flood in the Wilke Barre area of Pennsylvania. This was 1972 and Agnes was the first named of that year's Atlantic hurricane season ... and became, at the time, the costliest recorded hurricane ever to hit the United States.

Well, my father got in a boat and rowed, one by one, to the hospitals in our area ... looking for ways to help feed their stranded patients and staff. That story has always stuck with me. He made community involvement part of our Metz ethic wherever we happen to be.

Now this is how we ALL want to be

Every Friday – a "dress down" day at Metz – our people make contributions to a "Sunshine Fund." That fund helped one of our employees whose house burned down, for example. He had no clothes and our people's contributions got him things to wear.)

Last year at our annual Leadership Conference, as part of the event we had 340 of our GM's and Managers from 22 states all work together to prepare 75,000 meals for needy children and families in the Wilkes Barre/Scranton area. Sue and I loved giving our three kids their own first-hand experience of putting people first as they, too, helped with these meals.

One more example. Recognition is important in any family, right? If you ever got praise as a child for a good report card from school, a piece of art you'd worked hard at, an athletic win, whatever – then you'll remember from early on how meaningful it is in a family, as in life, to be recognized for something positive you had achieved.

Well, Bill Allman – General Manager for us at Lebanon Valley College in Annville, Pa. – created value cards for immediate recognition of any of our associates doing something great. That individual receives thanks and recognition on the spot – with her/her name on the card that comes with a reward. Versions of Bill's idea are now in wide use throughout our organization.

And most of our GM's make it a point to join their local Chambers of Commerce … not just because it's "good business" but also because contributing to one's community is a beautiful way to live.

Kindness and Respect is "Contagious!"

There are MANY examples of ways that Metz people show caring for each other and for their local communities in the ways we live our lives at work and at home each day. And certainly for our partners and guests.

But what I'm absolutely sure of is this: if our people didn't RECEIVE caring and respectful treatment each day, they wouldn't have as much spirit and motivation inside them to "pass it on" … to be considerate and thoughtful of others.

And as I said at the start and as I fervently believe, this way of treating employees – being concerned for THEIR welfare and wellbeing as a #1 priority BEFORE asking them to focus on clients, guests, community, etc. – makes a genuine and powerful difference in how they perform on the job each day.

Big corporation or family owned business like mine? People ARE people, and we have found that it pays to put your own people FIRST ... so they know and appreciate how it feels!

***

To contact Jeff:

President & CEO

Metz Culinary Management

Two Woodland Drive

Dallas, PA 1861

jeffm@metzcorp.com

1-800-675-2499

Admin. Assistant: 1-570-674-8788

David Norris

David Norris is a banker, outlaw biker, Rotarian, husband, father, grandfather, leader, and served as an Infantry Officer in the United States Marine Corps. He has extensive experience in leadership positions in both the corporate world of banking and the volunteer world of Rotary International. David is the former Chief Operating Officer of Happy State Bank headquartered in Amarillo, Texas where he worked for 24 years and continues to coach, teach, and mentor employees there.

David continues to study with and be mentored by many of the great thinkers of our time including Paul Martinelli, Mary Morrissey, John Maxwell and Les Brown. David is a Founding Member of the John Maxwell Team and as such is a John Maxwell Certified Leadership Trainer and Coach. Continuing to study under Mary Morrissey, he is a Life Mastery Consultant with The Life Mastery Institute. He has studied under Les Brown and is a Les Brown Platinum Speaker.

David is now a full time executive leadership development coach. His passion is leadership development and helping others to find and realize their dreams thought his speaking, coaching, teaching and mentoring.

IS IT GOOD TO BE YOU?

By David Norris

I have been saying that it is good to be me for some time. The truth is that it is good to be me. I am very good at being me. Nobody in the world is as good as I am at being me. I get to do lots of things. I go places, meet wonderful people, and have the most amazing friends and relationships. These relationships span the globe and for one reason alone……I choose it.

And while it has always been good to be me, I didn't always recognize how good it was to be me. I was victim to the mental games of comparison and validation and along with many other paradigms and ways of thinking to which we subject ourselves. Never good enough…Try harder…Good things come to those who wait…Better safe than sorry…Look before you leap…Don't do that…What will the neighbors think?…Who do you think you are?…Money doesn't grow on trees.

It wasn't until I chose to overcome being average or being mediocre and instead choose to live a life that is abundant, noteworthy, successful, and significant that I began to see how good it was to be me. It all started with making a decision… a decision that I AM worthy and deserving to have the life and lifestyle I want and deserve.

Perhaps my story is like yours. I decided on a career path to follow as I prepared for my future after graduation from college. A career plan that had me thinking this was the answer to my eventual success personally and economically. First, I learned the skills required to be the best Marine officer I could be whether that was putting steel on the target or loading a battalion of men and equipment on ships to travel across the Pacific Ocean. I expanded this skillset learned in the Marine Corps when I began my career in banking. My early lessons in leadership translated to expanding the skillset of lenders, operations and front line people to make my organization the best in its market. Doing the skills of banking better than the other guy in a largely commoditized industry is essential to the growth and prosperity and longevity within the organization. What I didn't realize was this was only one dimension to a greater path every individual must engage in if they truly want to live a life of abundance. A life of abundance is what everyone should strive to accomplish. In accomplishing abundance you will live a life that is noteworthy, successful and significant. Abundance is much more than a monetary goal. It includes health and wellness, relationships, vocation, and time and money-freedom. To live an abundant life you must follow a personal growth plan. A personal growth plan is mindset transformation to a mindset of abundance.

The development of a different mindset is not a new idea. In the 1800's people such as Ralph Waldo Emerson, Henry David Thoreau, and Louisa May Alcott would sit around a table and discuss a life unimagined by many. The basis was changing their mindset. Time and time again we see companies fail or fade away while others grow and prosper. Companies and organizations that prosper have the best leadership at all levels. They consistently maintain their relevance in the marketplace and consistently produce, grow, and develop their people. This is because the companies not only work on the business aspects of their organization but also the mindset. These companies understand that if their employees do not have the right mindset both individually and corporately they will not achieve abundance. The Bible says we are not to be conformed to this world but be transformed by the changing of our minds.

I can pinpoint the day my world was transformed. It was July 25, 1995 when my CEO gave me a book titled <u>Developing The Leader Within You</u> by John C. Maxwell. We devoted one officers meeting per month to studying a chapter. In 2000, I was elected president of my Rotary Club and was introduced to another John Maxwell book, The 21 Irrefutable Laws of Leadership. At this stage in my personal growth I was awakened by Law #2 The Law of Influence. The Law of Influence states "Leadership is influence, nothing more, nothing less and everything rises and falls on leadership." In that chapter Dr. Maxwell writes about CEOs who ask him what they can do to determine the leadership potential or ability of their employees. Maxwell tells them to get them involved in leading volunteers. When you lead volunteers you only have your ability to influence others going for you. There is no paycheck to dangle over their head, nothing but you and your own influence to see that a volunteer organization's goals and objectives are met.

The idea of influence so inspired me that I made the conscious decision to be the absolute best Rotary Club President that my Rotary Club had ever had. I had been in Rotary 17 years going through the motions of doing the Rotary thing without ever being a Rotarian. Having started on a path of personal growth, I no longer chose to follow just what was required but to step up and ask "this and what more is required to flourish?"

I attended President Elect Training and my eyes were opened to the deeper meaning of Rotary. I heard many great and inspiring speakers and met the incoming President of Rotary International. I found this organization was truly making a positive impact on this world and that had a positive impact on me. More importantly, I met some fellow Presidents Elect that were very dynamic and giving people. A couple of them were single moms, raising a family on their own, giving back to their community. They were big time givers to The Rotary Foundation. The Rotary Foundation provides funds to fight disease, hunger, and suffering worldwide. I had participated in many Rotary Foundation fundraisers but never had I made a contribution outside the fundraising events. How were they able to do this? I was embarrassed and ashamed of myself and took action. I could do better.

At the end of the year I was named the District's Rotary Club President of the Year. My club membership grew. Thirteen members, including me, donated $1,000 each to The Rotary Foundation. What makes this more important to my story is that this was the second time I had been selected to serve as president of a Rotary Club. I served my first Rotary Club as president 14 years earlier. I attended President Elect Training then and heard many of the same things. The difference was the lens through which I viewed my relationship to the world around me. I now viewed it through the lens of my personal growth plan. My mindset had changed to one that taught me that we are put on this planet to make a difference.

In 1991 I began work at Happy State Bank. I was in charge of bank operations. The bank was under new ownership and at the time, out of 880 banks in Texas, Happy State Bank was #812 with just over $20 million in assets and two locations. Today, Texas has over 650 banks. Happy State Bank ranks at #27 at this writing. We have 34 locations in 24 different communities and over $2.5 billion in total assets.

We grew slowly at first, planted a few new branches in nearby towns in the Texas Panhandle and in 2004 embarked on the first of nine mergers and acquisitions. The CEO "hunted them down". My job was to "kill 'em, clean 'em, and cook 'em." That is, I was tasked with leading the team making the data processing conversion, mentoring the employees of the new bank to operate as a Happy Bank and assimilating the new employees into our culture. I was tasked in leading a corporate mindset change.

It was 2009 and Happy State Bank had just crossed the $1 billion in total asset mark when I was asked to serve as a Rotary District Governor. As a governor, you are one of 530 people in the world of 1.2 million Rotarians. It is a daunting task involving two years preparation and one year of actual service with a lot of travel. Most people simply will not do this at all and doing it while fully employed is considered insane. I was insane. The challenge here is that during that three year process of becoming district governor, Happy State Bank would grow another $1 billion to $2 billion and complete four acquisitions. This tasked my leadership, our people and infrastructure.

I did not know how my new role as Governor was going to mesh with my work at Happy State Bank. I did know my bank culturally and historically and knew growth and expansion was in our DNA. I also knew I had a great team of leaders at Happy State Bank and Rotary that were there to support me. I felt there was high probability it could happen by choosing to allow my mindset to expand further to accomplish the tasks. I succeeded. During the busiest part of my tenure of District Governor, in March of 2012, I was promoted to Chief Operating Officer of Happy State Bank.

So what is the point, the matter, the issue, to this rambling? The point is most people accept what life gives them and settle for an average or mediocre life and simply will not step up to live the life they imagine because they are not aware they can. There is no quick fix to experience personal growth. It is an ongoing process of learning to accept your potential for greatness.

I have said several times that I chose to raise the level of my awareness as to my own leadership ability and potential. It would have been considerably easier to quit Rotary, or wait until I retired, or had more time, or not do it at all. Rather, I chose to step up and step into a life of my choosing. I chose to advance my life rather than retreat from it. This is what a personal growth plan is all about. Great and amazing things can happen when you consciously choose to expand your mindset and decide to raise your own potential.

During my post military career, I did what so many of us do and continue to do, to work, slave, and grind it out daily seeking to better our lives and the lives of our families, willing to accept whatever conditions and circumstance come our way, and glad to have a job. Undoing and unwinding decades of paradigms and bad habits takes time and gut wrenching mental work. I did not do it by myself. I did not have the ability to do it myself. All I knew was I wanted to grow. I wanted something better. Having coaches and mentors to show me the way was necessary.

Yes, I read a few books. These books were the catalyst; however, what really happened is that I made a conscious decision to develop my plan of personal growth and take charge of my own personal development and live the life I chose to live. I chose to grow as a man and as a human being and not be a human pinball with everybody in the world having their own flipper.

I associated myself with some of the greatest minds in the world. I sought to study with and be coached and mentored by them. These great minds include my friend Paul Martinelli, Les Brown, John Maxwell, and my coach and mentor, Mary Morrissey. It is through their expert guidance and my decision to invest in myself that I accomplish the things that I say I want in life.

I placed myself in a position of permanent discomfort. So many people, when confronted with the discomfort of their own personal growth and development run back to their comfort zone. Attempts or efforts to grow are met with fear and they allow themselves to be pulled back into the herd by people close to them because average people have a vested interest in keeping you just like them.

The biggest thing my coaches and mentors taught me is to be grateful. Gratitude is the most important lesson because without it there is no growth. Without gratitude I am unable to receive any of the many blessings and grace God has given me and shown me.

- I am so grateful for my wife, Candy, and daughter Andi, and my entire family, especially my granddaughters.
- I am so happy and grateful for the United State Marine Corps and the opportunity to serve this Country and grow as a leader and as a man

The Change[16]

- I am so happy and grateful for Happy State Bank and the opportunity to work in a place with people who share the same core values, where growth is modeled and expected, and who encouraged me to pursue my endeavors in Rotary.
- I am so happy and grateful for Rotary for the opportunities to serve and make a difference in the lives of others, in particular fighting hunger right here in America and traveling to India to help rid that country of Polio.
- I am continuously grateful for everything including bank examiners, crabby customers, pushy arrogant people, and poor leaders because they helped me grow.

You see, I am on a mission and that mission is to be the absolute best version of myself so that I can make the world the absolute best version of itself. Athletes, top business executives, and entrepreneurs don't get to the top of their games without training plans and coaches to help them be just that, the best version of themselves regardless of their conditions and circumstances. So many people say "I don't have the money" or "I don't have the time" or "I have to work". Those are conditions and circumstances used as excuses to not take action and remain stuck.

A person that really wants to grow, and truly wants to improve his or her life by creating an abundant life for him or herself will make the conscious decision to grow and develop themselves. They will do what they can, where they are, with what they have to reach their goal or dream. You are your most important asset. If you do not invest in yourself, why should anyone else?

Personal growth and development only requires a commitment to oneself. It does not require a person to quit a job or wait until a better job or environment or business comes along. Personal growth does not require waiting until the kids graduate or until you retire at some predetermined age or waiting until the economy improves. It only requires that you act now, in the present, wherever you are and doing what you can with what you have....and be continuously and constantly grateful.

Personal development and growth takes intentional commitment to this work and staying connected to this work. If you really want to grow, if you really want to prepare yourself for that promotion to the C-Level suite, if you really want to start your own business, build that dream home, or find that soulmate, start where you are, do what you can with what you have AND get a coach or an accountability partner. Engage in studies and mastermind groups to help you navigate your journey.

Do what I did or find what works for you. Just make some room for yourself. Be responsible and accountable to yourself for creating new space for new opportunities. Stop watching television and read a book instead. Unsubscribe from that daily digital distraction known as email and take action to stop them rather than letting them accumulate. Listen to audio books in the car rather than the radio.

There is opportunity for personal development everywhere if you just create room for it and exploit the opportunity when it comes. The opportunity is already there for you so have the courage to dream big about the life you would love to live. Take an action step every day even if it is a baby step and at the very least believe that I believe you can do this. You will soon discover that it can be as good to be you as it is good to be me.

***

Learn more about David Norris and his work at:

www.goodtobeme.com

davidnorris1976@gmail.com

806-679-9326

https://www.linkedin.com/in/superdavenorris

https://www.facebook.com/Superdave1954

Josephine H. Wilcox

Josephine is a self-taught entrepreneur. She came from a small farming town in Michigan. Josephine shares her personal story of overcoming the challenges of identity loss through trauma. As she persevered without any formal education as a successful Realtor and a Bridal Boutique Owner, you will find her noteworthy and uplifting.

You will begin to relate to Josephine and cheer for her as her story unfolds. She suffered through early childhood trauma, sexual abuse, illnesses, and near death experiences. Josephine is now embarking on a career as an Inspirational Speaker, Life Coach and Mentor. You can't help but notice how her experiences has given her the uncanny ability to help others on their journey.

Broken to Butterfly

By Josephine H. Wilcox

Growing up in a small town in Michigan, with seven siblings, feeling very alone, my first childhood memory set me up to persevere through devastating struggles which later proved to give me the strength to become the woman I am today.

"I hid in the closet, my cocoon, with my hands covering my ears, gently rocking back and forth praying that the abuse would stop. If I could just fall asleep in that dark closet with my "special friends" only I could see, they were always there for me. I was a frightened little girl, with eight siblings, and angelic friends".

My Father, a "hard working" man, though I learned strong work ethics from him, I also learned dysfunctionality from his abuse with alcohol. I remember hearing my mother scream as he would drag her through our house, and the evil look in his eyes I will never forget. I never shared this with anyone and though I shared a room with three of my sisters, I continued to communicate and rely on my angels, my guides, they protected me and gave me light. I didn't know at the time this was a gift, a special gift only I could call upon. Have you ever felt there was a higher power, or a sense of strength given to you from an unknown source and yet you are not afraid of it? This is how I grew up and how I live my life today, knowing with absolute clarity we are not alone, even in the darkest of times, we can use our minds and tap into a higher power to find the answers we're searching for. Even in a family such as mine, with no expression of love or affection, when we need it the most, if we're open to it… it's there for us. And I needed them.

As I developed through childhood and my teenager years, I became incredibly independent. I was abused, molested, and the target for bullies. I always felt a sense of shame and it held me back from asking for things I needed. My outlet was working and finding a way to pay for the things I needed. In my cocoon I found my can-do attitude, with a sense of vulnerability. At the early age of fifteen, my innocence was selfishly taken away from me. My parents never questioned curfews, dating or rules of any kind. Yet I was forever changed. I had no idea how deep I buried this until I was married with two children. Children have a way of showing you what happiness is. I was able to put perspective on my past and after much reflecting to find a way to be the mom I so desperate wanted to be, I noticed that so many others suffered as much if not more than me. This meant I was not a victim, and I could re-invent myself to become whomever I wanted to be!

I decided it was time to start my career in real estate to give my family a better life than what I had experienced. Isn't it amazing when others rely on you to provide for them, even though it wasn't a learned behavior for me, it came naturally to want to give them everything I possibly could. I pulled from this feeling, this need to change the pattern of which I lived and show my children what a true work ethic is and why it is so important. My guides would instinctively help me through this process too, even though I continued to question myself and my feeling of lack of acceptance and approval, I also found the strength to show up in my own life, setting an example for my children to do the same in theirs. I didn't know it at the time, but I was through my actions letting people know I didn't need their acceptance and approval, I only needed it from myself. Once you realize that no one has the power to control you, confidence becomes an action to draw upon. It's a mindset that allows you to not worry about what others think, because you simply must do what you have to do!

My adult life has been riddled with illness, accidents, abuse. I suffered from Grand Mal Seizures at the age of 38 and I have no recollection of any of the events caused by this disease. My heart had stopped as I was told I was, "Status Epilepticus" meaning they would never stop. Over a ten-year period, I suffered skin cancer, ulcers, gall bladder surgery, ovarian cysts, bowel surgery and so much more. I fell into depression and massive anxiety. I didn't feel beautiful or worthy. I recall being in this very dark place and hearing the words, "Fly Free"! As I finally decided to share my childhood suffering with husband, I recall his attention towards the television more important. This is when I made the decision *I AM NOT A VICTIM!!* I made the decision that he didn't know how to comfort me and that was ok. I also made the decision to leave and find my worth, doing the uncomfortable to discover comfortability. This is never an easy thing to do, but once you get through the sobbing, the feeling of failure, the release that all which has happened was not my fault, there is strength and freedom! You have dig deep within and forgive those which have hurt you, because they are miserable, forgive yourself for what you feel shame for when you did nothing to be shameful for, this is when you release all the bad, not for them but for YOU! This is where the price of freedom is paid, and you begin to understand, you are not broken, you may have been bent, but no one has the right to stop you from finding your wings and flying!!

My message to you, and anyone feeling shame from suffering by what has happened to you from other people is their lack of worthiness, not yours. You have the power within you to emerge from your cocoon and become your version of the most colorful butterfly!! And should you be gifted with the ability to hear your angels, and you are, pay attention they will not lead you astray.

Josephine Wilcox

***

To contact Josephine:

johelenwilcox@gmail.com

http://www.facebook.com/Josephine.Wilcox96

linkedin.com/in/josephine-wilcox-981339170

https://twitter.com/JosephineHWilc1

Dr. Tianna Conte and Rev. Azima Jackson

Dr. Tianna Conte

Tianna is a trailblazing blend of mystic, scientist and international bestselling author of Love's Fire Trilogy. She empowers people in personal evolution and enlightened self-care. Her career spans forty years as a naturopath, interfaith minister, shaman, and psycho-spiritual therapist in energy medicine.

She is the founder of a signature program, GPS (GodSource Positioning System) Code™ in collaboration with her beloved husband, William, in spirit. This feminine based spiritual system supports each person to navigate life's challenges in five simple steps, re-awakening divine guidance and innate soul powers. This access silences mind chatter and releases reactive emotions, showing a way to living life to the fullest.

Rev. M. Azima Jackson, MS, DMin

Azima uses energetic healing, song, meditation, counseling, and ceremony for life's rites of passage. This leads to greater self-discovery and re-invention. She is an ordained Interfaith Minister who holds a Doctorate in Ministry, Masters in Divinity from Yale Divinity School, and Masters in Biological Sciences. Chopra University recognizes her as a Vedic Master. Azima is well versed in both Eastern and Western approaches to music. She is a certified leader of the improvisational organization, Music for People. She has produced two CD's, *Passages Through Light* and *Angel Love*. Azima is Director of House of Light. She conducts retreats in CT.

Extraordinary Journey

Dr. Tianna Conte and Rev. Azima Jackson

"Those who are awake live in a state of constant amazement."
Buddha

What do the words, "extraordinary journey," mean to you? What images or wisdom come to mind? Are you enjoying and relating to your life as extraordinary? For us, the word "extra" stands out and becomes extra-ordinary.

What we know to be true is for an extra-ordinary journey there needs to be something extra. What do you believe goes into the extra? For us, the extra is living beyond the five senses. This is living as if the mind was a sixth sense as noted by quantum physicist, Fred Alan Wolf, in the movie we produced, Awaken Your Riches. This awareness was exemplified super-naturally by Tianna's NDE (Near Death Experience) and by Azima's mortal encounter with death. The polarity of these experiences became the foundation of the messages and principles that Tianna and Azima are here to share. The essence is in accessing the guidance and invisible power that is available to all of us.

Everything is perception. It is our perception that can keep us small or beckon us to evolve. Everything is energy as proven by quantum physics. Many have heard...."glass half empty, glass half full." Einstein states it best, "There are two ways to live: You can live as if nothing is a miracle; you can live as if everything is a miracle."

Are you aware of the magnificence of who you are? To perceive oneself through mere mortal eyes of body limited by skin boundaries and brain limited by thoughts and beliefs taken from pre-birth to age eight would be a travesty. Intuitively, as children we all engage in the magic of possibilities. Unfortunately, for many this is conditioned out through well-meaning parents and authorities who want to raise us to the ways of the world. They project their limitations on us as if they are the experts. The biggest fallacy is now continued.

We are here to erase the limitations placed on us and take back our divine destiny as stated best in the words of the French philosopher, Pierre Tielhard de Chardin, "We are not human beings having a spiritual experience. We are spiritual beings having a human experience."

We are bigger than we appear to be. We are talking about beings of frequency that are beyond what we can experience by the five senses. Tianna intuitively knew this, and her near death experience (NDE) in 1995 proved it to her. Without getting into the details, her NDE was not through accident or disease. It was through a body wrap meant to de- stress. This story can be found in <u>Love's Fire: Beyond Mortal Boundaries</u>. Hearing the following words, and an invitation to a life review, forever changed Tianna's perception. Her life was enhanced indelibly. Our desire is to enhance your life, as well, without the need for a NDE.

> *"Birth and death are the same. One is celebrated and one is feared. One is celebrated because it is known; one is feared because it is unknown...but both are about essence. One is essence taking on form and the other is essence leaving form behind, returning to Oneness. But both are the same.*
>
> *The period of time between what is birth and what is death is called life. It is about experiences, experiencing many things, unfolding the truth of one's nature, of expanding awareness of who you really are and the gifts you bring...discovering that love is a frequency, not an emotion. Only love is real. All else is appearance, a part of the illusion created by the senses, and the illusion of separation. Each person is in physical form to give and receive love and so therefore expanding the truth of one's being.*

Soon after the above words, what proceeded to unfold was a review of my life. It started from pre-birth and spanned the years to my present age. It came in the form of movie vignettes. I experienced each event of agony— not necessarily agonizing pain, but a painful memory. I experienced what I had felt, what I had thought about it, the choices and decisions that I had made— all of it. However, this is where they had an uncanny twist. I witnessed the memories with no judgment, as if I were watching the unfoldment of a perfect script.

As if by divine magic, light penetrated these memories, almost dissolving them. This light uncovered a picture far greater than my mind could have fathomed. Somehow the light of that presence shone through to reveal that each occurrence held within it a gift that was greater than the pain of the experience. As such, these memories of agony could be viewed as growing pains. Indeed everything, bar none, served...regardless of my own judgments....Every one of my experiences had a purpose in some divine design....I feel confident in saying that those moments that cause the greatest pain can also contain the seeds of our spiritual awakening. "

As a therapist and shaman, Tianna realized that as we go over and over the pain of our life story we solidify its limiting beliefs rather than releasing them and triumphantly transforming them. What we need to do is experience the pain fully and release it as soon as we are capable. Her quest became the desire to pass the gift of a life review on to others, without the liability. Not knowing or getting logically caught up in the "how to," she trusted that all would be revealed. Eventually she met a doctor whose audio CD's addressed the issues in an effortless way. This became the first piece of the puzzle.

Together they designed a journey that is a cross between a vision quest and a life review, empowering people to shift to a foundation based on life enhancing beliefs. Since each person is unique in their memories and experiences, the work is customized, and takes them from pre-birth, through the birthing experience, childhood, culminating in Maslow's hierarchy of basic needs fulfilled in the present.

As the universe would have it, the gifts of the NDE continued to manifest and pass on to others in ever expanding ways. Clearly ensconced in the knowing that all is frequency, and we are that, a friend introduced Tianna and Azima to a computerized energy based machine. This energy machine uses modern technology and an ancient prayer modality, known as the Tibetan prayer wheel, to access the benefits of a higher frequency and divine possibilities. This tool is used to take one's intentions, to release subtle energy blocks, and to send blessings and prayers for transformation. This technology works with a full-length photo of the person requesting balancing. It bathes your picture with vibrations that first clear and then balance your energy field as it subtly

reduces stress. As we were writing this, Tianna realized that the energy machine is the closest to duplicating, on autopilot, an invisible power to dissolve the blocks that blind one's perception of the divine blueprint, similar to her NDE.

Tianna's "aha" moments continued as she realized another piece of her NDE puzzle had unfolded. She had recalled that during her NDE she was bathed in a Light and frequency of Love that was beyond words, and "the peace of God which passes all understanding" (John, Bible). Upon hearing this Azima was inspired to mention the quote from 1 John in the Bible, "God is love."

At this point, Tianna played with the words she heard in the NDE. "Love is a frequency, not an emotion." For the first time, she expanded it to say, "God is a frequency, not a religion... God is Love". This awareness rang true for both of them, and they became humbled in its message.

The famous quote of Rumi came alive,

"I belong to no religion. My religion is Love.

Every heart is my temple."

To our amazement, as we continued to craft this chapter, we witnessed the biggest piece of the NDE puzzle come into visibility. Despite her hesitancy, Tianna felt pressed to express the memories of the trauma and tragedy that happened when she was thirteen years old. The essence, without the details, is that Tianna's father (her hero, doctor/mentor) died, and she was sexually violated the same day by a trusted relative. We both recognized that this sacred wound was crying out to deliver the ultimate message that Tianna had heard energetically and never understood ("In time, Truth will be revealed.").

Although the young Tianna had raged in agony at the force called God during her darkest hours, she had been embraced by an energy of Love that filled her with an ecstasy of Light. It was similar to that experienced in her NDE decades later. She had also heard, for the first time, the voice of guidance as a loving power that she affectionately related to intimately as God. The first words were:

Surrender Each day Step by step

> You will be shown the way" (<u>Love's Fire: Living the Awakened</u>
>
> <u>Journey</u>)

Speaking and listening to this voice became a daily discipline and undergirding to transforming Tianna's life from tragedy to triumph! Accessing this awareness became the foundation of a life's calling that spanned forty years of empowering others through her gifts. Her longing had always been to set people free from self-imposed limitations and dependency on outside guidance.

This force had mystically aligned Tianna to perceive and live life from the inside out. She realized that most people were conditioned to live life from the outside in. Her burning desire became, "How could this wisdom and transformational shift be passed on?" The humorous answer to her prayer was through the bite of a poisonous brown recluse spider on our land in Costa Rica.

As Tianna's healing journey progressed with a combination of minimal medical intervention coupled with innate wisdom, a system emerged. Each day, as she peered and applied the cream and gauzed the deep holes in her toes created by the spider's poison eating to the bone, a vision appeared. One step, each day for five days, followed by five more days of hand signals and gestures, and a seeming miracle unfolded. Not only were Tianna's toes made whole, so was the code made manifest for others to take their steps with a simple blueprint for guidance and power. The same words Tianna heard at thirteen could be duplicated for all!

We are honored to introduce this system, affectionately called the GPS Code. The acronym, GPS, is **God-Source Positioning System** for those who are comfortable with God as a frequency of Love: for others, **Guidance Power System.**

We grappled with revealing the 5 gears and hand signals at this time. As Azima and Tianna continued to dialogue, what emerged was an awesome awareness that the seed to the GPS Code was hinted at in what Tianna heard mystically: "Surrender, Each day, Step by step, You will be shown the way." We marveled that the daily discipline and two of the five gears were obvious in this quote. At this point it was evident that it would not be in the highest and best interest of you, the reader, to get a sketchy look that could not be easily applied.

Yes, they are called gears for a greater reason that takes you beyond steps. The gears appear simple, yet are significantly more than they appear to be. If you desire a deeper understanding and fuller experience of this **GPS Code,** we are thrilled to take you to your next level. Please visit https://www.yourgpscode.com and enjoy the trip called evolution!

We can assure you that by setting your innate GPS your soul will be in the driver's seat of your own vehicle. As with your car, this system will set your destination to the best solution of your problem, shifting you from self-sabotage to self-empowerment. In the words of Einstein, "When the solution is simple, God is answering."

One of the undisclosed gifts that Tianna received in the NDE is that the chatter of her "monkey mind" was silenced. Passed on through the GPS Code is this ability to quiet your mind, as well as a simple way to release your emotions so they are expressed rather than repressed or suppressed. In essence, it's about shifting from reactive living to responsive living for an extraordinary journey.

Feeling fulfilled at a level that defied her conscious mind, Tianna embraced that her NDE had given her the pieces for a sneak peek into the bigger picture of her life. As Azima listened to these profound revelations she was awestruck and speechless. Tianna urged her shocked friend to be patient and compassionate with herself. Azima, and in turn, connected with her heart to express her truth. The starting point for Azima was her affinity and guidance through music and sound healing.

As we discoursed and mused over the expansiveness of human consciousness, a memory came up for Azima. She remembered her

Indian singing teacher once describe Indian music as having no beginning and no end. While *22* notes are audible to the physical ear in Indian music the intervals between these notes are microtonal. Her teacher had referred to entering worlds in these minute intervals, or vast states of consciousness, psychological and emotional, where the music took her. If we look at life as vibration, the reality is that there is no beginning and no end. We both saw this as a metaphor for life.

The Change[16]

We acknowledged that sound could be the bridge between form and invisible energy, between the manifest and the abstract. Azima's Indian music teacher further saw music as a path to self-realization. As we explored this possibility the following quote came to mind, "In the beginning was the Word, and the Word was with God, and the Word was God" (John, Bible) . Azima realized that if one sees God as vibration, as the frequency that breathed and continues to breathe us into existence, then it would make sense that sound/music would be a pathway to our authentic Selves.

She took a quantum leap in her own evolution by realizing that God is beyond form, beyond masculine and feminine. An ecstatic Tianna chimed in, "Anyone that gets this understanding, sets themselves free." At this point, Azima referred to a quote from her mentor in spirit and Sufi mystic, musician, Hazrat Inayat Khan, "They have said that the soul entered the body through music. In private, they have said that the music itself was the soul."

Azima began her own conscious review of how important music had been to her since childhood. In so many ways it had been her gateway to her soul's guidance. As Tianna pressed her for more information, what started to unravel was the story of Crohn's Disease and how Azima nearly died several times. Although Azima admitted that medicine helped her, she eventually began to be more frightened of the medicine than the disease itself. So she began looking for alternatives or complimentary modes of healing. This is when her spiritual journey began to expand and the following poem emerged:

> I woke
>
> In burst of light

To see Love's perfection A glimmer of eternity

> In you

As the pain of the Crohn's Disease deepened so did the writings and the music. The turning point piece that Azima was hesitant to share was the Angel song in which she had first felt the palpable love of angels. At that time she was not ready to share the song because it had an intimacy and love to the likes of which she had never experienced before. She didn't want to lose that visceral knowing:

> Angels surround me, enfold me with love
>
> Hold me and fill my heart with light and
> love from above. Their wings encircle me
> bringing their peace
>
> Comfort, protect me
> bringing their peace.
> They're with me
> always, in this I rejoice;
>
> They're with me always, in this I rejoice (<u>Angel Love</u> CD)

In retrospect, Azima realized that her physical sickness was a portal opening for her into higher dimensions. It wasn't until many years later that Azima recognized that Crohn's disease had been suppressed emotions that had not been acknowledged, and continued to eat away at her until she began to face them. To listen to her cells, her needs, was part of her journey. This listening took different forms. Music was one.

Because music is vibration, it has the ability to connect directly to the frequency of our emotions. It can release emotions of pain, fear, anger, and bring harmony and peace to one's cells. For Azima, playing an Indian string instrument, the tamboura, and often chanting with it, released pent-up tears. As she continued this form of prayer, she felt nourished by their vibration. So much so that the accumulation of these chants became a CD (<u>Passages Through Light</u>) for others to enjoy as well as to imprint them in cellular memory.

The Change[16]

Is there a musical instrument that you play or music you enjoy, or chants that would evoke thoughts, emotions, or body sensations for you? What would they be? For Tianna classical music, especially Pachabel, came to mind.

Sounds also affect us in different ways. Toning and humming are simple methods that you can access anytime you need. These can support you to get in tune with your body and emotions: centering and lowering blood pressure are also benefits. This particular exercise activates the brain, and cleanses every fiber in the body and brain.

It is a basic humming exercise.

> Sit in a relaxed position with your eyes closed Purse your lips as if making the sound, "shhhhh"
>
> Hum loudly creating a vibration, particularly toward the front of your face
>
> Hum a single pitch continuously
>
> Imagine you are a hollow reed filled with vibrations of humming At some point you will become just the listener; the humming will
>
> be happening by itself
>
> You can do this until you feel a shift

Another powerful form of vibration is chanting. A Tibetan abbot once had talked to Azima about this, and described it as prayer in which the feeling of the chant, with repetition, brings the person to a vibrational level where the request has already been answered.

For Azima , music continues to be her pathway to her soul's voice and to setting her free. In the words of Hazrat Inayat Khan, "Music touches our innermost being and in that way produces new life, a life that gives exaltation to the whole being, rising it to that perfection in which lies the fulfillment of one's life."

These memories had Tianna and Azima sometimes laugh,

more often be amazed, at the opposite directions that they have lived into life, into their soul's nature. Tianna, since she was a little girl, had a more energetic, mystical perception of life. Experiencing death through the eyes of a NDE even anchored Tianna more toward the mystical point of view. Azima, on the other hand, in a more physical human way, came close to death at least two to three times, and felt only pain, with often little hope. This anchored her into the struggle of the mortal point of view. We agreed that the dance between the mystic and mortal perceptions embraces the totality of life.

We trust that we have imparted wisdom from our extraordinary journey to empower the "extra" in your journey. Our message is that as we each awaken to who we truly are as infinite beings of Light and Love, we are here to live fully and leave a lasting legacy. In opening our mind and joining in the union of our heart, we raise our consciousness. This opens the gateway to the alchemy of personal and planetary transformation that is the ripple affect of awakening and an extraordinary journey for all! The words of Lao Tzu exemplify it best:

"If you want to awaken all of humanity then awaken all of yourself. If you want to eliminate the suffering in the world then eliminate all that is dark and negative in yourself. Truly, the greatest gift you have to give is that of your own transformation."

***

To Contact us:

For Tianna:

http://www.yourgpscode.com

www.spiritualitymadepractical.com

drtianna@gmail.com

www.facebook.com/gpscode

www.facebook.com/Tianna.Conte.77

www.linkedin.com/in/drtianna

(914) 205-4969

For Azima:

www.ahouseoflight.com

www.maryazima.com

https://www.facebook.com/maryazima

https://www.linkedin.com/in/mary-azima-5796bb10/

info@ahouseoflight.com

(203) 643-8033

Pamela Church

Pamela Church is co-founder of Bank for Wealth.

She and her husband, Bruce, were what most people would call rich. Then, everything changed. Bruce was laid off his corporate job where he had been making a lot of money. It felt like their own personal financial crash.

They feared losing their horse farm and the lifestyle they were used to. Pam and Bruce decided to become entrepreneurs thinking that it would help us create our own wealth and financial freedom, but we were still burning through savings quickly. It takes money and time to get a business going.

She realized that the ability to make money and the ability to manage it were two completely different skill sets.

They weren't doing what the truly wealthy do. They do something different. Very different. That's how they stay wealthy, by working smarter, not harder. Pam and Bruce learned how to handle money differently and decided to create Bank For Wealth to teach others to do the same.

Bank For Wealth helps people learn how to handle money the way the wealthy do to increase savings, increase security and provide a future for generations to come.

Financial Shift

By Pamela Church

Do you have a big enough passion to help you change the way you look at wealth creation instead of just getting by?

I used to push money away without realizing it and most people do the same thinking it's evil. For you to welcome money in your life, the first thing you'll need to know is how money really works.

My God-given passion to work with horses on a deep level surprisingly has been a key in creating wealth in my life. The catch is, when you decide to create wealth, it forces you to change by learning what you don't know, and finding your 'blind spots' to become better.

I remember my journey started when I was 5 years old. I snuck out of the house to go see a horse I had noticed many times while riding in the backseat of my parent's car. Sneaking out that day, meant I had to overcome any fears and become courageous.

One night, I tried quietly sneaking out of the house using the front door, but the door made a noise awoke my mom, so I scurried back to bed as to not be caught. My parents were separated at the time, so seeing the door open and thinking there was a potential burglar frightened her. Right away, she called the police and then my dad. When he arrived and peaked in my bedroom, I was relieved he didn't catch me hiding under the covers fully clothed. My parents never found out it was me that opened the door that night.

Determined, I woke up before dawn the next morning and this time, I left out the back door. I walked up the road about half a mile before realizing the neighbors leaving for work would see me and tell my parents. In that moment, fear set in and I quickly ran home to make sure no one ever knew I was gone. Fear was probably a good thing at this point, just imagine a 5 year old out roaming the neighborhood at sunrise!

My deep desire for horses became the motivation to position myself in a better financial situation than parents were. My passion for them led me to big changes and one change, was learning how to treat my hard-earned income differently.

Like most people, I wasn't taught much about money growing up. The only thing I knew by the time I went off to college was to keep my check book balance above zero.

If you haven't seen the animated comedy, "King of the Hill," it's about a family from Arland, a fictional Texas town. The show's families basically work a regular 9 to 5 job, drink beer at night, tell crude jokes at the dinner table and live for the weekends. In a lot of ways that show reminds me of how I grew up in my small Texas town.

Looking back, I realize I was living circumstantially without planning for my financial future. All I knew, was that I'd go to work, work hard, and live for the weekends. As far as buying a horse farm, I figured that I'd search for the best paying jobs and work as hard as I needed.

I find it funny looking back now, but when you are brought up a certain way for 18 years, you have no concept of how much more there is outside of your current life experiences. At that time, it's obvious my subconscious was running my future and little did I know that I needed to change my mindset to learn what I didn't know to grow.

When I left home, my life as a young adult was based on what I had been taught or not taught. I didn't know what I didn't know, and two of those things, sadly, were how business and money really work.

The Change[16]

I grew up in the 80's blaring rock-n-roll in my car with the windows down. I used music to entertain myself when things were tough or seemingly impossible as a teen. I never thought about becoming better or looking for ways to grow through pain. For instance, when I figured out my family would never be able to afford to buy me a horse, I put that dream aside and got into things like concerts, dancing, and anything that would make me feel better emotionally and even spiritually.

I thought focusing on being happy was all life was about, so I did things to promote that and became quite self-absorbed. I didn't think about helping others, just about surviving and having horses, which led to a materialistic way of life. At that time, living by circumstance instead of planning for tomorrow was common. Maybe you can relate?

There were five of us, me, my two siblings and my parents. We were a middle-class family and while both my parents worked, money was often tight. Being able to afford anything other than the basics was not a reality. The reality was, my parents worked hard and were disciplined in saving for retirement. They put their money in a company plan or traditional retirement programs, which left little extra to spend on us growing up. Family vacations were few, but we did have an above ground pool and a big back yard, so I chose to find contentment and happiness in that. I knew I would do the same and just work harder to be able to have a horse farm one day.

My parents did what they knew and did their best to raise us with the information they were taught growing up. They gave us a "good" life and some of my childhood experiences having less, made me a part of who I am today.

When it came time for college, I had not even planned on it until a couple of months before I started. I'm grateful my parents wanted more for me than to just graduate high school and work for minimum wage. They told me I needed to get my college degree to have a better job.

In college I took economics and some business classes, but I still knew nothing valuable about money. Half-way through college, I was paying for it on my own while I worked to earn an income. I had no problem working hard to get what I wanted, which was being able to afford a nice house, a nice car and the basics. Horses were not on my mind at this time because I set that dream aside. For a long time, I thought owning them was out of reach.

Life was still good. I was young with lots of energy and ambition. I would do what it took to live better than my parents who both worked and would partied on the weekends as a stress relief. My first experience with getting what I wanted outside of paying my rent and utilities was when I bought my first new sports car in my early 20's. That was the start of my mindset shift, realizing I could earn more and be upper middle-class if I chose.

When I met my husband, Bruce, we were both working in sales selling office products. He was selling fax machines when no one had them yet and I was selling copiers. When I was out working to find potential customers, I would come back to the office with fax leads, which I handed over to my soon to be husband. We both joke that I brought in the leads and had to marry him to have advantage of the commissions paid from the sales.

Bruce and I got married and we knew we had to find good paying jobs to live above average. We both enjoyed the idea of having land and building our perfect home with a swimming pool. We were very focused on living the lifestyle, but not understanding how money really worked. Then the passion for horses I'd put aside years before started to blossom again.

We were both making incredible income for our age. Bruce held a great job in medical sales, and me in real estate, so one day I told him I wanted to get a horse. A year later, we had 15 of them! We both had 401K's that seemed to be our ticket to retirement and we were investing in risky things to get even further ahead. More on that later. We had built our dream home by our mid- 30's and we felt we had 'it all.' Then, we decided to start a family. That was the first big change in my life that forced me to start paying attention and thinking instead of doing things on a whim.

In the past, I was living by circumstance and working hard. I got lucky and landed a real estate job that paid me very well. Now, with our first baby, I 'retired' from working.

Looking back, I remember me quitting work wasn't just based on being a stay-at-home mom. There was a point when we calculated our incomes and concluded it wasn't worth me working to be in a higher tax bracket. If you think about it, thinking about having to pay higher taxes because you're in a higher income bracket isn't going to create wealth without more knowledge about money.

Again, we were living based on emotions instead of planning for tomorrow. Paying more taxes means you're making more money, so we needed to find a way to pay less of them instead of giving up working. This is called tax avoidance and not tax evasion. The wealthy do it.

> *"Anyone may arrange his affairs so that his **taxes** shall be as low as possible; he is not bound to choose that pattern which best pays the treasury. There is not even a patriotic duty to increase one's **taxes**. public duty to pay more than the law demands."*
> *Learned Hand*

Like most, the reason we were not inspired to figure out how money really works was because we didn't know any better. We were also young and 'invincible,' and figured we could make up for lost money from risky investments by working harder. I had planned on going back in real estate and making lots of money again to catch up after my son's graduation from homeschool.

Well, there's a law called Parkinson's Law which caught up to us. This meant that our expenses started surpassing our income. We were living luxuries that were now essential with 10 horses and our new Colorado dream farm.

Here's how this happened... Shortly after moving to Colorado to buy our beautiful horse farm, I learned about network marketing and it opened up my eyes to a different way of working. I was thinking that maybe I didn't need to work weekends in real estate to catch up with inflation and retire early.

I was excited about what we'd been shown with building residual income, and Bruce was enjoying the extra income I was making at the time. Our horses were an expense that we didn't pay close attention to, but it felt good to provide some of the income. (He does help me pick up manure in the pasture though, so he's a great horse lover's husband!)

Again, we were continuing to live for today instead of building for tomorrow because the money kept coming in and we were keeping up. During my time homeschooling our son, I focused on raising him to be an entrepreneur. I saw a better way for him to work and have more control of his life earlier than I had. I also raised him to become strong at being self-taught in areas he wanted to learn. Everything seemed to be going well for our family and even more so because we came out ahead selling and buying our homes.

Then it happened, we had financial issues and were on a budget for the first time! Shortly after our move to Colorado, we got the news that Bruce was being laid-off. I thought the news was good because I was committed to us both working from home and building a bigger network marketing business. Bruce wasn't on board selling pills like me but went along with my enthusiasm to change.

The Change[16]

Network marketing started us on our personal journey to entrepreneurship. Working harder to get ahead mid-life, we invested over $100,000 to help us change and become successful entrepreneurs.

Over the next 4 years, we would go through some of the hardest times of our lives. We were using our savings to figure out what we'd be doing with life part II while dealing with failures and mistakes. It was a difficult journey, but we learned from it. We were committed to living with purpose in our life instead of just working for a paycheck, but there was more to learn for that to happen.

Then, I learned to work smarter not harder after reading "A Four Hour Work Week." The problem was, I started operating on fear-driven ambition trying to figure out how to make more money to replace Bruce's high salary. All without working 40+ hours a week. I knew we could make great money because we'd done it before, but it wasn't happening fast enough. Our expenses were rising to meet our income quickly and I couldn't figure out how to work smarter.

I started wondering if Bruce should go back to what he knew, but my drive to not give up on a better way of working kept us going. A friend told me that not giving up is a characteristic and sign of a true entrepreneur, so I kept up the pace. It wasn't until I was in my 50's that I figured out that money is spiritual and that relationships build wealth. Only problem, we still didn't have the secrets of the wealthy.

Through my persistent reading and investing in my personal growth, I found the most important thing we needed to be doing and it's what you need to do too. It's amazing how many don't know about the 'legal secrets' of the wealthy. We found it by:

Being uncomfortable

Reading a lot of books

Getting mentored by those who'd been where we'd been and succeeded

Failing forward fast

Learning about financial information even when we thought we were in no place to invest any more money

Taking action quickly

Our biggest problem was not knowing how money really worked and how to hold onto it. I didn't understand this part until I decided to start seeking out the answers. One mentor told me, "If it sounds to good to be true, then that's when you ask questions."

Our minds finally opened up to learn how to keep our financial security from depleting. It was frustrating thinking about how much money had gone through our hands that we felt we'd now lost control of.

Here is what I've learned about creating wealth:

Learn how to use the velocity of money instead of letting it sit in a savings or traditional retirement program.

Build secure wealth before investing in more risky things.

Grow your money tax-free

Find a guaranteed way for your money to grow.

Save, be disciplined, and delay gratification more.

Learn the 'legal secrets' of the wealthy.

When we found what the wealthy were doing differently, we decided to make it our work. There's a huge gap in what people don't know, so we are closing that gap by doing education seminars at no charge. We are passionate about helping other entrepreneurs who are serious and will take-action to build their wealth. It has become our labor of love and our business.

Now, I specialize in teaching business owners, professionals, and executive's secrets the bankers don't want you to know. In fact, if most people understood money the way bankers do, they would think about and utilize it differently. The vast majority of the population has deliberately been sold a set of beliefs by bankers and Wall Street to keep them content. We teach you: understanding the velocity of money, growing money tax free, growing a retirement plan without the restrictions, taking more control over your money, taking risk off the table, what the big banks and elite do with their money (Hint: It's not what you think) and using their strategies to grow your money guaranteed. I believe in giving power back to the people. We work with people who are committed to getting outside the box, creating wealth, and are serious about making a change.

***

www.BankForWealth.com

https://www.linkedin.com/in/thepamelachurch/

email: contact@bankforwealth.com

https://www.facebook.com/bankforwealth/

303-660-1771

Venetia Zannettis

Venetia Zannettis is a Law of Attraction Expert, Neuro-Linguistic Programmer, Hypnotherapist, Subconscious Re-programmer, and Master/ Teacher Healer. She is a recognized authority in achieving groundbreaking results. Venetia has served as a guide to individuals around the world, and as well as seeing clients on a one-to-one level, she also offers a variety personal development and self-healing online courses. Venetia has a unique gift of positively transforming the lives of people and is well known for her ability to turn ordinary people into extraordinary individuals. She has empowered many through her work in creating positive thinking patterns, removing emotional clutter and childhood traumas, changing limiting belief systems, and deleting faulty subconscious programming. And as well as guiding individuals toward healthy self-talk and self-empowering behaviors and habits, she teaches the art of inner peace, joy, balance, and well-being. She delivers seminars on how to create the life of your dreams using the law of attraction and the subconscious mind to break through the unconscious blockages that sabotage your happiness and success. On her mission to impact the lives of many, Venetia has dedicated her life to raising the vibrations of humanity by guiding them toward love consciousness bringing them to a state of pure happiness where miracles happen and dreams come true.

Stepping Out of Denial into My Truth

By Venetia Zannettis

My name is Venetia Zannettis and I was born into a poor Cypriot family in North London in 1979. I was the youngest of three sisters until my younger brother was born six years later for which I was happy. Throughout my childhood, my parents struggled financially. They worked in a shoe factory from morning to night just to make ends meet, and their lack of control over their money problems put extra stress on them, thus the family. My father liked to drink and socialize with his friends. He was the head of the house and whatever he said was final. He was also prejudiced against women and this hatred for women was inflicted continuously upon me as I was growing up. Throughout my childhood, I remember feeling unworthy and unloved because I was a girl. My mother was the servant of the house who lived a stressful life with many concerns. Her job was to keep my father happy while taking care of four kids and all the chores around the house. Due to my parent's financial struggles and many other issues, our family home environment was anything but loving and affectionate. My parents argued constantly and my mother would regularly cry. Our family home looked like a normal household from the outside but hopelessly sad inside.

I began secondary school at age eleven. After school, my siblings and I would head straight to the shoe factory to work with my parents until late in the evening before heading home where my mother would cook and clean and my siblings and I would start our homework. Eventually, this lifestyle began to take its toll on me. At school, my grades were terrible and I became a straight D and F student - I adopted a rebellious nature and would even skip classes. I started to build up a lot of resentment, anger, and hatred toward my family and society. I was miserable and hated my life, and at the age of thirteen, I run away from home. I remember traveling for hours by bus and train to get as far away from my family as possible. Late that evening, I was found by a social worker sleeping on a bench outside a train station miles away from my house. The very next day, I was sent to a foster home. The first night at my new home, I sat in bed in the dark and cried for hours - this was a sorrowful time in my life. I started to build up a lot of fear, mistrust, and self-worth issues. Two months later I went back home to live with my biological parents but nothing had changed. Resentment was running free on both sides which led to even more anger inside my family home. From then on, the relationship between myself and my parents was terrible and it wasn't long before our relationship turned vicious.

Some months later, my entire family and I moved to Cyprus in the attempt to live a better life, but I hated living in Cyprus as I had left behind the only school friends I had. I became uncontrollable and would continually run away from home. Each time my father found me, he brought me back, but I would run away again. Late one evening, at the age of fifteen, I run away for the last time. This time, my father never came to find me which is what I wanted. I hitched a ride to another city far away. I had no money, no friends, and no idea where I was going or what I was going to do. That same day, I got myself a job as a waitress which I thought would solve my problems and bring happiness into my life. Boy, was I wrong - within a few months, alcohol and marijuana abuse became a part of my daily life. At the end of the workday when I stripped off the Band-Aids of fake happiness, I had no choice but to feel the hurt of my loneliness and insecurities. The wounds were exposed and it felt awful. And alcohol helped - until it didn't. Eventually, I started drinking at home alone before leaving the house which started to induce a depression-like behavior in me. So, why was I drinking and smoking so heavily? Well, these substances suppressed the fear, resentment, hate, and insecurity that I held within for so long - they hid my lack of self-worth, lack of self-love, and lack of self-confidence. Little did I know that this self-destructive lifestyle was the beginning of a ten-year uphill battle with heroin and crack.

Two years later and heavily hooked on alcohol and marijuana, I was sexually abused which piled-up on my already existing dysfunctional life. I continued to go from disaster to disaster and my life was falling apart before my eyes. After years of self-abuse, the pain was so unmanageable that I turned to even more self-destructive methods to alleviate the distress. I started hanging out with toxic people who fed my addictions, who were inherently bad for me, but at the same time, provided me with temporary relief from the constant hell I was experiencing. We gradually began experimenting with heroin and cocaine until experimentation became a substance use disorder. I became so addicted that my entire life revolved only around heroin and how I would get my next fix. I became dissociated from myself and from the world around me. This addiction cost me my job and I could no longer support my habit. In my desperation, I began smuggling small amounts of drugs from a foreign country as they were cheaper abroad. And I did this many times. It was not long until my house was raided and I got arrested for drug possession and faced with a possible five-year prison sentence. As I waited for the verdict, my time in custody was agonizing as I suffered from excruciating physical pain, migraines, vomiting, and fainting due to severe drug withdrawal. However, I was released eight-days later with the firm condition that I sought professional help. Upon my release, my parents insisted that I move back home with them, and although I didn't want to due to old unresolved hurt, I did because I had nowhere else to go.

For the next two months, I was on and off drugs. And then suddenly, one evening, I was the victim of an unfortunate car accident. I remember waking up in a hospital with facial injuries, severe drug withdrawal symptoms, and deep depression - I felt exhausted, lost, lonely, and a failure. And although I usually kept a smile on my face while secretly suffering, I could not hide it anymore - my fake happiness pilled off and I felt terrible. And due to this unfortunate car accident piling-up on my already existing dysfunctional life, I contemplated suicide. The depths of the fear that I felt on that day were so brutal. It was the first time in my entire life that I felt so out of control and terrified of what I might do to myself. And as I feared for my life, I signed myself into a psychiatric institution and from then on I was in and out of hospitals.

Some years later and in complete desperation, I moved back to North London with a family member to start drug treatment programs but nothing worked. Instead, I overdosed many times. I hated that my family saw me in this uncontrollable state, and although they were very supportive, I still abandoned my family home due to overwhelming guilt, shame, and indignity. And that's when I found myself homeless on the streets of London where I remained for two years. I slept on street corners and abandoned sheds, and during the harsh winters, I even slept in waste areas to keep out the bitter cold weather. Late one winters night, as I took shelter in a garbage dumpster to rest for the night, I remember attempting to sleep while sitting upright due to the infestation of maggots on the walls eating away at the garbage slime. I remember the scratching noises as they feasted away, and although I felt disgusted, my despair and tiredness overruled the discomfort of crawling worms. To survive on the streets, I turned to shoplifting which got me imprisoned twice. Upon my release, I returned to Cyprus for therapy with the financial help of a family member. For six months, I was taking prescribed medication which made me worse than ever– I began to feel extremely depressed. The antidepressants were not helping me but rather making me worse and that's when I began struggling with suicidal thoughts.

I was exhausted as I felt I had tried everything, yet nothing was working, and that's when I reattempted suicide by pills. I woke up in a hospital in complete hopelessness and desperation. I didn't know anything anymore – I hated myself. So why didn't I ask for

The Change[16]

help as I felt my life crashing down on me? The answer is fear, guilt, and shame, the most dangerous combination. I feared that if I opened-up to anyone about what was happening inside my mind, no one would understand. I also felt guilty about pushing the weight of my sadness onto others. But most importantly, growing up I was taught that showing emotion was a sign of weakness and for this, I was ashamed - ashamed of being a young girl who was so depressed, desperate, and weak. For this reason, I put on my ''who cares' attitude and continued to suffer in silence. Sometime later, I woke up in a state of such intensive panic. Negative, disturbing images were stuck in my brain, perpetually haunting me. I couldn't eat. I couldn't sleep – that was my first anxiety attack.

My life was slipping away before my eyes and I couldn't do anything to stop it. I was living in a vicious vortex of sadness and misery – an agonizing slow-motion suicide. And to make matters worse, my poor family, who were filled with fear, were suffering with me. And that's when I realized that I had to make a major life choice - change or die. I knew that my life depended on me making the right decisions and taking the right steps toward recovery. I knew that to survive, I had to begin the hardest journey of my life – the journey to find myself. I also knew that on this journey I needed to keep hope alive. And that's when I had a moment of sudden realization. "This is it - it's now or never," I said to myself. Right there and then, I took a huge leap of faith into the unknown journey of recovery. And for the first time in my life, I simply trusted that everything would work out for the best - that's when my healing journey began.

I began soul-searching and reading self-healing and personal development books. I did a lot of research on the power of the subconscious mind and the Law of Attraction. I began to realize that we can't think negative thoughts and expect to live a positive life. We can't think thoughts of defeat and expect to live in victory. And after coming to this understanding, I knew that my job was to restructure my brain for positivity while simultaneously, eliminating the old ways of negative thinking - and this became my intention.

First, I pictured the version of myself that I wanted to become and the type of life I wanted to live. I imagined in vivid detail what exactly that version of me looked like, how she thought and felt, how she spoke and behaved, then I went to my current self and asked, ''What am I not doing that-that person had to do to achieve that level of excellence? What must I do within myself and my surroundings to become that person?'' And then I begin doing those things daily without excuses. Every day, I raised my personal bar to uphold that standard. I started observing my thoughts, feelings, words, and actions so that I can begin to live from true choice in the present moment rather than being run by programming from the past. I stood guard at the door of my mind to catch my thoughts, and every time I caught myself dwelling in self-destructive thoughts of misery, I immediately shifted my focus to self-empowering thoughts of love, happiness, peace, and well-being. By doing so, I was slowly restructuring my mind for positivity.

I also worked hard on transforming negative feelings that haunted me for years. For example, every time I found myself drowning in undesired emotions such as anger, fear, sadness, guilt or shame, I instantly jumped up, changed my body posture and breathing pattern and indulged in fun activities to encourage positive feelings such as tennis, dancing, or painting. This was not always easy and nor did it come naturally, but I made sure to do it anyway. And by doing so, I slowly began to feel more alive. I continued to observe my speaking habits. Every time, I talked negatively of myself or others, I immediately created positive talk and expressed myself lovingly. I stopped saying I can't and started saying I can. I stopped saying I am sick and started saying I am healthy. I stopped saying I am weak and started saying I am courageous. I used positive affirmations to send messages to my subconscious mind describing how I wished me and my life to be. And as I spoke lovingly of myself, I was slowly becoming a positive communicator. Furthermore, every time I caught myself taking negative action, I immediately changed my deeds to positive that strengthened the new me. I observed how I reacted toward different people and situations and entertained only behaviors that served me. I made sure to always operate from a place of love and purity. Bit-by-bit, I was taking positive action and making my life better. And the more I acted from a place of love, the more my actions lead me toward a loving place. And finally, I carefully constructed a new nurturing lifestyle that supported the new me. I created a lifestyle filled with truth, love, joy, peace, balance, and harmony by staying away from pessimistic people and situations that got me down. While simultaneously, surrounding myself with happy, upbeat, feel good people that lifted me up.

The next six months was the most challenging transition I have ever encountered and despite my many setbacks, I'd managed to make improvements in my life. Day-by-day, I was stepping out of denial and into my truth. I was regaining balance and vitality. I was transforming negative habits and rituals to positive. I was restoring my mental, emotional, physical, and spiritual well-being. I was piecing myself together and becoming whole again, and it felt great. I started looking. I searched every corner. I tried new things. I got uneasy, I get scared, I become a beginner again. I questioned everything, I evaluated my life and my place in it. I found subjects I knew nothing about and learned them well. I did anything and everything that was the opposite of what I did in the past. I failed miserably and then I tried something else until I found myself. I learned something new about myself every day; not only about my character but what made my soul sing and my heart dance. I kept going until I laughed again, until I discovered understanding, acceptance, happiness, joy, and most importantly, purpose. I searched until I found what turns on my light. And finally, I found something that turned on my light, I found purpose. I found pleasure in healing, in therapy, and in public speaking - that's when I fell in love with me.

My transformation seemed so magical, so enlightening, and so much needed at the time. Clarity entered my life as a light shining in my path. I began to experience significant transitions in life and I loved it. Such a transition was beyond my comprehension, and until today, I can only explain it as a miracle from God, from the Divine, the Creator or whatever you like to call it. I knew right there and then that I had started a new chapter in my life and for this I was excited. I continued to go from strength to strength. I taught myself to read and write fluently, and began blogging for two Cyprus magazines and was awarded Best Blogger Award for spreading positive energy to the readers. That was the least I could do to give back to society.

Two years later, I met the love of my life and with his financial help, I enrolled in a Psychology course and qualified in Emotional Intelligence. I continued to go from one accomplishment to another. Since then, I have studied a variety of healing modalities and qualified as a Master/ Teacher Healer. I later received my diploma in Neuro-Linguistic Programming. I continued my studies and trained as a Hypnotherapist. From then on, I opened my practice and saw clients on a professional level. I found joy in guiding people toward uncovering their inner power, achieving a positive mindset, improving the areas of life that matter the most, and in cases like mine, creating a total-life transformation. Today, I deliver intensive seminars on the power of the subconscious mind, the law of attraction, and constructing the life of your dreams. And as well as seeing clients on a one-to-one, I also offer a variety of personal development and self-healing e-courses to improve yourself from the comfort of your own home. Today I am very happy with my life and I love who I am. And my message to you is: Have faith, never give up hope, and never give up on the dream you hold in your heart because dreams come true when you believe.

***

To Contact Venetia:

Social Media: Venetia Zannettis

Website: VenetiaZannettis.com

Email: Venetia@VenetiaZannettis.com

Michelle Gesky

Michelle Gesky has 20 years of experience in consulting, training, executive and personal coaching & development as well as business operations. She is a Certified Relationship, Leadership, Health and Wellness Coach, Speaker and Author. Michelle is an intuitive and compassionate powerful coach, committed to generating that her clients live authentic, purpose filled joyful lives full of possibility.

Michelle held senior positions at Franklin Covey as Senior Client Partner, & at Judlau Contracting as Manager of HR/Training and Development. She was Vice President of Strategic Relationships at Global Performance Solutions for many years before being hired as General Manager at Launch, a NYC post production house in Advertising. Previously she was in the Investment Banking Division at Goldman Sachs in HR/Leadership Development & Training working with the Managing Directors and experienced hires. Consulting assignments included Fortune 500 Corporations and small and mid-sized companies in a wide range of industries. After years dedicated to business professionals in the corporate arena she is now living her passion by empowering her clients to dig deep, get curious and shine brightly with exuberance freedom and power in their own lives. She loves to Kayak, paddleboard, travel, spend time with her three children and her dogs.

The "Sh#*%" Word

By Michelle Gesky

Have you ever noticed that there are some things we just don't talk about? In fact, there are things we don't like to even think about. Those things have the power to plummet us into deep, yucky, feelings and thoughts, which include, guilt, fear, overwhelm, hopelessness, lack of worth, experiencing our self as not good enough, defective, different, alone.

I have coached thousands of clients over time and one thing that screams to be discussed but which gives people the Heeby-Jeebies, is anything that causes us to experience the S word: Shame. We don't like to hear the word repeated, right? It makes us uncomfortable to think about someone else feeling the S word! Uh oh, and what about ourselves.?!!!. We'd almost rather chew on glass. You may be thinking about skipping this chapter right about now, just so you don't have to read further, right? "I'll deal with it later" we often think to ourselves. "I don't have time for *this* "(this being an opportunity to get into closer relationship with your very own personal shame) ... Maybe you're thinking that you don't have a problem with it… hmmm could be... But it could also be that you don't give yourself - permission to acknowledge that more than likely shame lives within you awakening when you are in the throw of an unhealthy dynamic. Like the monster under our bed as children that we were so scared of, we fear and dread shame. When I was a child we were told not to say the world "Hell', as if saying it would bring the devil, horns and all, to pop up wherever we were. My clients have always resisted discussing shame, or any topic which triggers shame as we work together. Shame is, to use an analogy, the devil in the room with us.

Shame is a five letter word, but we have more fear about speaking about shame then we are of saying that Four letter word we are all so familiar with. I can relate and through much of my life have tried to avoid shame at all costs, until I learned that shame is hard wired into us as a benefit, to help us survive as human beings. Shame can be a game changer.

Shame as benefit

Shame it turns out, is hardwired into our collective DNA, probably to keep us functioning as a society, tribe or family. Shame goes back to our primordial days perhaps when we survived by staying together against the elements- Dinosaurs? Harsh weather? Hard to find food or water? It was a basic survival lifestyle. Shame allows us to query ourselves, to correct, redirect and re-member ourselves with the people around us. Shame helps us to say "Is what I have done or not done, said or not said, something that I need to examine"? "Where am I misaligned with my values, my integrity, or the integrity of the group I'm in"? Shame helps to acknowledge something could have been handled differently. In our Dinosaur days, being able to access shame would have perhaps allowed someone to stay in a group, to survive rather than kicked out into the wild, alone to face potential death. In that way, shame is healthy for us all. It is a definite diagnostic tool we can use. We must re-learn how to address shame when we are suddenly in the midst of it so that we are able to use it to move us forward instead of keeping us stuck where we are.

In my chapter on shame in "<u>Authentic Alignment, Wise Women Reveal the Secrets of a Stellar Life</u>" I posit that shame is analogous to an indicator light in your human programming system that shows something is awry within the heart of you. The operating system runs quietly in the background but sometimes programs need to be updated. As an adult you have the choice to use the new updated system (in this case, healthy shame) or the old one installed by your parents and society (unhealthy shame). The authentically aligned you is using the uncomfortable experience of shame to communicate with you. The heart of you is your authentic self, your center which steers you and is made up of your values, beliefs, assumptions and our true north, which some may call soul. When something occurs and it could be an outside event, action, dialogue or an internal self-dialogue that starts because we are judging ourselves, then we may be pulled away from our center and into what I'll call the old shame drama which distorts your perception of yourself and your situation. This is where shame takes center stage and ultimately steals the show.

"We don't see things the way they are; we see them the way we are" -The Talmud

Shame has two guises, healthy and unhealthy. The shame I described above with the Dinosaur lifestyle is the healthy shame, a little uncomfortable but powerfully re-directive if we know how to read it. When my clients learn to be deeply curious about shame's message, make different choices and learn from what it communicates, healthy shame is a wakeup call. If not, the unhealthy shame is an undertow pulling you out of yourself, away from your center, underneath the water where we experience the sensation of drowning in our emotions. The emotions are from our core beliefs, assumptions, assessments, and thoughts. Symptoms of unhealthy shame are the icky feelings: unworthiness, avoidance, humiliation, self-loathing, anger, sadness, fear of being abandoned, looking bad, being wrong, being confronted or found out. You may even perceive yourself as the mistake, rather than understanding, *"I made a mistake but I am not the mistake"*. Knowing this is the critical path to freedom from unhealthy shame. The reality is, if you can look below surface to your own internal self-mechanisms you can change your relationship with shame from unhealthy to healthy.

Our Interpretations create our Shame

Our relationship with ourselves is based on many things but with shame the most important is our relationship to our thoughts. Our thoughts are based on our interpretation of things and what we have learned to be true. This comes from childhood. These thoughts and core beliefs impact how we make choices in our lives today. Let's look at how it works.

Imagine if when you were very young, you saw a dog coming toward you. Suddenly, that dog got hurt. You might make a connection that when a dog comes toward you, it gets hurt. Therefore, you start to avoid dogs, not wanting to hurt them. The truth is that the dog getting hurt had nothing to do with you. This kind of collapse between two separate events into one and your inability at a young age to use logic creates an incorrect assumption. That assumption turns into a belief that you cause dogs to get hurt, and that influences your assumption about what to do the next time you are faced with a dog. All this may occur beneath your conscious thoughts; therefore, you do not necessarily recognize that these early childhood beliefs are part of <u>your always</u> having the feeling that you should avoid dogs! This creates a conscious choice to step across the street though you don't remember the reason why. Now as an adult you are wary of dogs!!! To sum up, in that example and in life, our beliefs and assumptions are often driven by thoughts or beliefs that may not be the truth. Our own beliefs, coming from the past, often drive our shame and so must be observed!

Integrating "Our thoughts create our reality" into your awareness moving forward is vital to freeing yourself from shame's grip. Once you can look at your thoughts and beliefs to see what is activating your shame & the emotions around shame, you can start to let go of the unhealthy shame energy.

The Anatomy of Unhealthy Shame

Some of the thoughts that encompass your experience of shame come from what you learn as a child from your parents, your church, synagogue, mosque, schools, society, etc. It's inauthentic because they are not your true beliefs but inherited. As a child you held peoples repeated judgments as truths, rules and regulations that governed you. Remember at the beginning of this chapter I mentioned that we are hard wired to feel shame to keep us as part of the pack? The reason we will experience these internal thoughts, judgment and feelings is that we remember them from our youth as the voice of adulthood, telling us how to correct our actions/inactions so that we could stay safe. Therefore, we would not get separated from the pack. We experience the voice of shame as a parental figure that we needed to trust. The messaging is unhealthy and painful but we feel it is there to protect us/love us. It is there to ensure that we are accepted by our parents and others. We therefore struggle as conscious adults to uncouple ourselves from our historical outdated voice of shame. Uncoupling ourselves from shame makes the inner child within the adult, feel out of control, and abandoned.

Most of us recognize unhealthy shame. We abhor the feeling and yet we feel it so frequently we are almost unconscious of it. When you look in the mirror, what do you say to yourself? What is the inner voice? Is it judgmental or critical, or is it telling you "hey, you are really beautiful/handsome today?" When we look in the mirror we are often not simply looking at ourselves but we are hearing the voice of shame (other people's potential criticisms and judgments). Often we have rapid, fleeting thoughts almost at the speed of sound. The only way that we actually know that they are shame based thoughts is that suddenly we feel mad at our self, have a moment of self-loathing, sadness, or feeling of alienation before we stuff it down. The thought happened so fast that we only mostly unconsciously recognized what it was saying. How many times have you walked by someone and you perceived them as silently judging you? In that uncomfortable moment, shame is taking the stage. You walk by them on the street for example and never see them again. However, the shame is vocal now and you can feel its presence in your demeanor, attitude, and perhaps even in its being experienced as a lack of self-worth, or through your anger.

Take a moment now to stop reading after this paragraph and start to ask the following questions. Doing so is a courageous act that will support you, bring you clarity and create positive steps toward a healthier relationship with yourself. When was the last time I felt shame? What does shame feel like to me? How often do I feel shame? Do I recognize my experience of shame for what it is or do I just judge myself and get angry at myself?

What is the worst part about my personal shame? How does it affect me? What are the behaviors I exhibit when I feel shame? What would I like to change in my relationship to my shame?

What did you take away about your relationship to shame? Can you tell if your shame is from your own internalized, but slightly awry thoughts and beliefs or is it the shame from younger days when you listened to the world around you for cues as to how to behave?

An example of how shame can affect you can be seen by taking a peek at an example from my own life.

When I was young my mother took me to a modeling assignment. I told my mom I felt ill. She thought it was nerves. I vividly remember to this day the experience of climbing on these big white cubes to stand on for the photo shoot with the bright lights on us, the darkness all around and the photographer saying "honey why are you so slow, you are the youngest, yet you are moving like a sloth". What's a sloth?? I only knew I felt like I was about to throw up. I said "I don't feel well" but the photographer and my mother ignored me. I threw up all over the cubes and on some of the assistants. I could feel the other models looking at me and I felt alone, outcast, criticized by the photographer. I felt shame. I wanted to belong so badly, I didn't want to do the wrong thing ... Why did I experience shame? In this instance I had outside help from the photographer and the other models judgments. But I also internalized it and judged myself unequal. Remember, our shame is personal and from our culture around us, like our families. My shame came from my parents always trying to avoid shame themselves. My dad was an attorney in a big old, white-shoe, Wall Street law firm. My dad started out poor, a foreigner, without connections. He felt he had to fit in, to make it there. My mom went from the city to the suburbs to raise me. She was a working woman. The ladies in the suburbs didn't work and mom tried hard to act and participate in the same ways the suburban women did. That was the strong subconscious message I had from my parents. Survival means looking good and fitting in, following the rules. You can see why I had shame at that age. My parents were already modeling looking good, fitting in and not breaking the rules and communicating it to me verbally and non-verbally.. I felt I didn't fit in, look good and wasn't following orders. My own internal sense of shame became activated. Except, remember, it really came from my parents/ need to avoid shame. It didn't originate from me, but it was within me.

So let me tell you how shame shows up now as an adult. Unhealthy shame appears as an indicator that I am acting outside the lines of my comfort zone and it doesn't feel good. My tendency is to hide. Instead I can choose quickly to rewire how I process that shame, choose not to listen to the old shame system but instead check in with my internal thoughts. I can learn what's really going on for me. I am gentle with myself looking for what I can do to move me forward in a shame free direction by taking immediate action. We are wired to feel shame. This is a benefit if you can uncoil the thoughts that don't serve you, the beliefs that are no longer relevant or true about who you are today. Our bodies are also designed to help us, in that our brains internal limbic system, which is the brains emotional dashboard can help us. A scientist named Dr. Mathew Leiberman discovered that using simple language to name our emotions actually quiets the arousal in our limbic system. So, talking about shame with someone trusted helps us quiet the emotional pain.

You are strong, resilient (hey you are still here, right?) you are multi-tasking in a busy modern world with many distractions. You are a good person who has made mistakes just like the rest of us. In essence part of our beauty is in our humility that we are not above or below others, that as human beings we make mistakes. Healthy shame helps us acknowledge that we all make mistakes and are hopefully learning from them. Healthy shame is there to guide as like a GPS to auto correct ourselves. Healthy shame is meant to keep us in integrity with who we say we are and who we want to be.

"Your time is limited, so don't waste it living someone else's life. Don't be trapped by dogma-which is living with the results of other people's thinking. Don't let the noise of others 'opinions drown out your own inner voice. And most important, have the courage to follow your heart and intuition"

Steve Jobs, Co-founder, Chairman, CEO of Apple Inc.

Tools for transforming your relationship to shame.

Start a gratitude journal. Center yourself for a few minutes each day to be present and tap into what you are grateful for.

Look ahead by creating a cup list (my version of the bigger bucket list) ... write down something you'd really like to do that would make you happy that is achievable each day or week, then take steps to accomplish one.

When you feel an unwelcome emotion do a shame check. Scan to see if it's the healthy updated shame operating system or the outdated unhealthy version. Be curious and gentle with yourself.

Take actions to support you by reaching out to someone you trust, or go find a mirror and talk to yourself. (It works.) Remember you are designed to speak about shame because then your brain starts to numb the pain!

Practice taking deep breaths, closing your eyes and do the following exercise from Authentic Alignment: Heart of Shame. Picture yourself when you were a child. Take a moment to experience it. Add yourself in now as an adult who wraps their arms around little you. Then speak to shame so that your little self hears. Something like -unhealthy shame I don't need you now and I will be responsible from now on, and protect myself." Tell the voice of unhealthy shame whatever you need it to hear. This helps little you un-attach from the unhealthy shame. Tell your critical voice that you are strong, wise, and you can never be alone because you love yourself. Speak your hurt and acknowledge your feelings as both the mature you and little you. Tell little you that he/she is loved and able to make her/his own choices safely. Check in with how you feel when you finally have said what you need to say and open your eyes.

***

To Contact Michelle:

Phone: (914) 471-5712

Website: Directimpactnow.org

Twitter: @Dune63

Facebook; https://facebook.com/MichelleGesky

Or ask her any questions at Michelle@directimpactnow.org

Asha Mankowska

Asha Mankowska, MA,Esq. is an Internationally Renowned Business, Executive & High Performance Coach, Branding Expert, Bestselling Author and Charismatic Speaker. She is a Keynote Speaker at prestigious universities (Harvard, Yale), conferences for leaders, CEOs, executives and entrepreneurs in USA & Europe. Recognized by Forbes Magazine as one of the Top Business and Career coaches in America. She accepted the honor to be a member of Forbes Magazine Coaches Council and her articles are featured in Forbes Magazine on regular basis. Her book "Ignite Your Life" became a bestseller in two top categories: sales and marketing. Asha was also honored as a Thought Leader & and Woman of Influence. in Hollywood.

After been an attorney for 11 years Asha made a courageous career change and the last 16 years she had grown multiple 6 Figures companies and helped her clients to do the same. As a Founder of business Mentorship & Mastermind: HIGHLY PAID EXPERTS ACADEMY powerful community for entrepreneurs who are ready to become influential Leaders, she addresses cutting edge concepts to implement and dominate clients' industry, position themselves as powerful and charismatic leaders, influence the world, and make a fortune by doing what they love with integrity and authenticity.

She was a Founder of Speaking Academy "Speakers Bureau for dynamic women entrepreneurs", the Podcast's Host "Crush Fears with Asha

Manifest Your Greatness Today

By Asha Mankowska

The foundation of our life is freedom to be, do and have whatever we desire. The perfect time to unlock our true power and rise above our circumstances is today.

— Asha Mankowska

Most of us have goals and dreams, such as, to be happy, financially secure, thinner, or fulfilled in relationships, but all too often nothing is done to make it happen. We think of things or conditions that must change *before* we start, and set our sights on *someday*. "Someday I will lose weight, get married or start my family or business." Using this approach 95% of people will never reach their goals.

My passion is to inspire those who have a deep desire to achieve their goals, those who are ready to make a commitment and take the necessary steps to turn their desires into reality. I want to inspire you to be in the upper 5% of the exclusive club of "Movers, Shakers and Action Takers"; to help you manifest your desires and your greatness beginning today. How many people do you have in your life that inspire and support your dreams and significance, and who can also provide you with the tools you need? Less than 5% of people have such support. I will give you the keys to unlock the powers that you already have in you, but which are for now, safely locked away. There are no conditions or special things to be done, obtained, or finished to start this journey — we simply start here and now. When you are ready to jump in with both feet, you will be amazed at what you can do.

Why Should You Thrive for Greatness?

Nowadays we have very comfortable and easy lives. With so many modern conveniences, we often don't strive for bigger goals. It is simply easier not to challenge ourselves. In fact, a culture has been created where we are happy with mediocrity, indolence and "no expectations". There are plenty of people content to live from pay check to pay check, and satisfied with the life of a couch potato. If that's a happy life for some, so be it. But that's not you. In fact, you could be a role model and an inspiration for others. My role is to ignite you to greatness, to lift you up and to activate your power to achieve. By power, I do not mean "potential."

Everyone talks about accessing potential, but for me potential is like the Loch Ness Monster: everyone has heard of it but no one has seen it. It's very enigmatic and intangible. Potential is the capability to develop something in the future, having skills, qualities or abilities, which may or may not be developed.

Power already exists in every single person. It's a strength and influence that we can enforce and execute. We can make things happen when we have power.

A person, who unlocked their power, has access to their true creativity and freedom, lives according to their dreams, is motivated to be their best every day. Your power, the essence of your greatness, is this fire and passion in you, this magnetic confidence that radiates from within, attracting positive attention without intimidating or diminishing others. It is also the calling to be someone with a higher purpose; someone who has a desire to be the solution, not the problem; who seeks out responsibilities and challenges; someone reliable who can deliver on their promises; who makes a big impact and leaves a legacy.

Detect, Confront & Eliminate The Major Enemies to Your Greatness

"F.E.A.R. has two meanings: Forget Everything and Run or Face Everything And Rise. The choice is yours."

Greatness means reaching further into yourself and achieving your goals. In order to manifest greatness, you have to be bold and courageous, shake things up and challenge the status quo.

Everyone talks about the perfect recipe for success. I am going to play devil's advocate, and talk about a perfect recipe for disaster. We all experience fear in life. Unfortunately, most people let fear, resistance, and frustration control their lives and stop them from achieving their dreams. They would rather stay in their toxic although cozy comfort zone, miserable, frustrated and feeling sorry for themselves, instead of taking the fear along for the ride and achieve whatever they want. It's incredible how people will do absolutely anything to avoid facing their fears. They will broadcast how much they want to achieve their dreams, and yet at the same time, nurture their resistance and all the "perfectly good" reasons why they can't achieve their ambitions. They run the risk of never getting what they want, and of being paralyzed by fear for the rest of their lives.

You need exactly the same amount of energy to stay in your status quo than it would take to remove the resistance and get what you really want. Just shift the direction. Fear creates resistance. Resistance is what our excuses are made of, and it is something that stops us from taking action and creates frustration and anger. These in turn create depression. Here are your steps towards failure:

Do not face and do not confront your fears.

Let fear draw you down into a life of resistance and inactivity.

Let this inactivity become frustration, unhappiness, and ultimately depression.

In fact, that is the perfect recipe for depression.

Fear is not real. The only place that fear can exist is in our thoughts. It is a product of our imagination, causing us to fear things that may not ever exist. Danger is real but fear is a choice.

—*Will Smith*

Distinguish fear from danger. Fear serves no real purpose apart from hindering our actions and progress. They are just excuses to procrastinate and create a protection for own ego, so its feels safe and unchallenged. Fear seems to "help" by making us avoid difficult circumstances. We use fear as an emotional crutch for our weaknesses. We might be afraid of being rejected, isolated, abandoned, but those are only social circumstances that we can overcome. Take public speaking, in surveys it's usually rated as one of the highest fears, second only to death. Yet public speaking can be taught, learned, and mastered.

Fear rips us away from greatness. While fear can destroy you, the good news is that you can also destroy fear. You are much stronger, if you only allow yourself to be. You can either live the life of your dreams or the life of your fears. The choice will always be yours. If we can overcome our insecurities and fears, we can be successful in anything. The way to do it is to shift from fear to freedom, because freedom is the biggest motivation there is. We already have it within us to overcome fear. It's time to stop playing safe. You don't need permission, acceptance or perfect timing to be brave or see what you are made of.

"*Our deepest fear is not that we are inadequate. Our deepest fear is that we are powerful beyond measure. It is our light, not our darkness that most frightens us.*" Marianne Williamson

The Steps to Manifest Your Greatness

Your life does not have to be controlled by your fears. It can be full of strength, passion, financial freedom—you can live your own ideal scene.

While I can show you the way, it is your choice whether to explore this path or not. I am not introducing you to anything new that you need develop within yourself—I am only reminding you of whom you already are. You create your own life and experiences. You already have that power for inevitable success. Here is the recipe on how to access your greatness, and to manifest everything you want, right now.

You can't solve a problem with the same level of thinking that created it.

—Albert Einstein

In order to become the solid rock of your life, completely challenge your way of thinking. If you want to see more kindness, love, respect, and greatness, you have to become that person! I hope to inspire you to leave behind anything that holds you back, eliminate fear and resistance, and help you recognize, access, and reactivate your own personal power.

Step 1: Make a Full Commitment.

"There's a difference between interest and commitment. When you are interested in doing something, you do it only when it's convenient. When you are committed, you accept no excuses, only results!" You have to be fully dedicated, focused and committed to achieve your goals. What you are willing to do and how far you would go to get it?

Step 2: Ask the Powerful Question.

In order to achieve anything, you need to tap into what motivates you the most. While people ask HOW, the most powerful question is: WHY? Your why is the motivation for your actions, especially when you feel tired, disappointed or overwhelmed. If your why is strong enough, the how is irrelevant. What's your WHY?

Step 3: Take Full Responsibility

Myth: We feel entitled to a life of happiness, an awesome career, nurturing relationships, and more.

Truth: there is only one person responsible for the quality of your life and only one person who holds the power to make it possible—YOU!

Accept full responsibility for your life, results, and circumstances, what you attract and experience.

> *You are responsible for your life. If you are sitting around and waiting for someone to save you, to fix you, to even help you, you are wasting your time.*
>
> *—Oprah Winfrey*

Summon the courage within and change things around you. Take back the ownership and control: from victim to victor. As a victim you feel small, vulnerable, debilitated, stuck or trapped, like you can't move on. But whatever has happened in your life take responsibility for it and for how you will act and react in the future, or you won't be able to achieve anything. When you blame others you let them dictate your reality. Give up all excuses, blaming others, explaining why you can't or you haven't. Develop the identity of a victor, so even though you face the same circumstances, they will no longer disable you. Are you taking responsibility for your life today?

Step 4: Unleash Inspiration & Support System

Do you know why these 5%, the Movers, Shakers, and Action Takers are so successful? They have a dream team of supporters, mentors, and coaches. Create your own team that will make you unstoppable, remind you of your greatness, challenge and believe in you. Are you reaching out to someone on consistent basis? I will be delighted to assist you in actively pursuing your dreams.

Step 5: Become a Magnet to Attract Abundance

The principle is: *like attracts like.* You are your own gateway to prosperity. The *law of abundance* says that there is an overflowing quantity of everything in this universe for us: the health you desire, all the money you want, fulfilling career and love. All you have to do is unlock and receive your abundance.

It's your choice: do you choose abundance or do you not? On a conscious level, everyone chooses abundance and prosperity. However, on an unconscious level, you may be repelling abundance and be unaware of it. Being truly successful begins with a state of mind, with thinking BIG. What's your Big Picture Vision?

Step 6: Open Up for an Effortless Flow of Prosperity

To be our own gateway to prosperity we have to develop the concepts of appreciation, releasing control and going with the flow. As soon as we start treating life like as a gift, we open ourselves to an overflow of more gifts.

I was taught I must work hard to achieve anything. Struggle, effort, and hard work were always a part of my former mindset. But the more I studied the mindsets of successful people; I discovered how to *effortlessly* speed up my achievements. At first, it seemed like a foreign concept to me. For all lovers of hard work, don't worry, superior performance is still required. There is no magic wand that will allow you to just follow a successful plan consisted of quick steps to get happy or instant gratification. Success takes consistent effort. It doesn't happen overnight. The truth is that you can't just substitute "working smart" for "working hard" and constant dedication. You have to do both. But action doesn't contradict allowing; it's a key ingredient.

When we are receiving we are in a "state of allowing". Allowing means to deliberately choose your thoughts, words, and actions, to allow yourself to align with your desires. The state of allowing isn't a passive surrender to the universe, a state of inactivity and laziness. It's a state of inspired action, strategy and deliberate focus; a state of non-resistance that creates a momentum for the universe to act for you. You are the decision maker. You are telling the universe which direction you want your life to go. Allow the universe to play its role, provide the signs, people, opportunities, which will allow you to achieve what you desire. There is an ultimate balance between acting and receiving which creates *flow*. Going with the flow is a perfect way to accelerate our achievements. Do you know how to recognize WHEN to release control, let the universe work on your behalf, and receive?

Step 7: Manifesting Anything You Want

Everything is achievable. It depends on you showing up at your best in the world.

When you want something, the entire universe conspires in helping you to achieve it.

—*Paulo Coelho*

We are born with the ability to create a life of total fulfillment and the power to control our destiny. We do this by influencing our thoughts, emotions, and actions. Our thoughts and emotions create our reality. We can bring to us whatever we desire, because everything we think, feel and believe has energy. This way we attract and manifest a similar energy. If you are depressed, full of fear and resistance, guess what you attract into your life? When you believe in your own power and take responsibility for your own actions, you attract more wealth, health, and happiness.

Sometimes people believe they are too old to start something new, such as going back to school, getting married, starting a new business. Brian Tracy couldn't pass high school English, is now one of the top-selling authors in the world. Colonel Sanders, the founder of KFC, did not become wealthy until the age of 55.

What determines whether we live the life of our dreams is simply if we unlock our power. Once we envision it and *own* it, no matter what, we can manifest it.

Here are four steps:

Ask

First decide what you really want. Don't live someone else's dream—it will show by your lack of passion, dedication, and commitment. Instead, *reclaim your own power!* You deserve to have everything in your life exactly the way you want. Make a list of your dreams and turn them into a plan of S.M.A.R.T goals:

Specific

Measurable

Achievable

Relevant

Time bound

It's like activating your inner GPS. Decide what you want and ask **as if** you expect to get it.

Believe

Those who win are those who think they can.

—Richard Bach

You get what you expect, so believe in yourself and go for it. It's an attitude: failure is not an option. After deciding what you want, request it, and *believe* that it will be answered. Your belief must be so strong that you don't worry about *how* it will manifest. Just like after you input a destination into your car's GPS system, you don't worry about *how* you will get there.

Receive

This step is the most overlooked! The biggest enemy of receiving is resistance. How fast you manifest your desires depends on how deeply you believe you can achieve it, and how effortlessly you allow it to come into your life by removing resistance and create a space. As soon as you make room in your life, your desires will have space to appear. In order to get more of what you want, you simply need to get rid of what is no longer useful. Did you clean out your garage for your dream car, make time for new clients, or space for your soul mate in your life?

Action

"The distance between your dreams and your reality is called action".

Planning and strategizing, is great, but nothing will happen until you actually take action and implement. Most people spend their lives waiting for the perfect time and perfect conditions to start something. Studies prove successful people act, get results, and jump on opportunities. Unsuccessful people get the same ideas, have the same information, but they come up with excuses rather than taking action. Quit waiting around and get into the game now. Work your plan and never give up! We are being measured by our actions not intentions. What bold actions are you going to take today?

The Power of Now

Things might come to those who wait, but only the things left by those who hustle.

—Abraham Lincoln

When we wait for things to happen, to be delivered to us on a silver platter, or depend on things outside of our own control to change, we diminish or surrender our own power. Summon and activate the courage you have within. Take back ownership and control of your life. Be accountable for who you are and what happens to you. You will then inspire others to be on the top, successful 5% with us, initiating greater change.

We already hold the keys to our greatness inside. You have to find your unique way to activate and unlock it. This is the truest adventure you can have, and I would be honored to help you. Let's enjoy the journey! Success comes to those who don't settle for less!

***

To Contact Asha:

www.yourfavorite-lifecoach.com

Asha_Mankowska@yahoo.com

619 471 6932

Facebook: https://www.facebook.com/pages/Asha-Mankowska-Your-Favorite-Transformational-Life-Coach/219849214774401

LinkedIn: https://www.linkedin.com/profile/view?id=173194011&trk=nav_responsive_tab_profile

Google+: https://plus.google.com/u/0/115390807162601572872/posts

Twitter: https://twitter.com/AshaMankowska

Mark Recker

Mark Recker attended college after high school for a year but was drawn towards the higher paying auto industry. He applied and tested for a skilled tradesman apprenticeship earning him a Journeyman card in the mechanical trades in record time. He later thirsted for more knowledge and attended a few more years of college studying business administration.

Mark is also the successful inventor of an exercise apparatus that received a United States patent. His creativity as an out of the box thinker did not stop there as he applied his talent towards building successful down lines in network marketing. His passion for problem solving and helping others succeed has earned him the respect as a true leader in the network marketing industry.

Mark's real passion though is his love for network marketing and helping others succeed. He currently sits on the advisory board for a Health and Wellness company that markets nutritional products that aid in adult stem cell production and weight loss. Mark, credits his success to his work ethics and responsibility he learned while growing up on a 600 acre farm and his competitiveness in High School sports. He enjoys being outdoors with nature and relaxing on a beach.

Biography of Entrepreneur Mark Recker
By Mark Recker

The #1 Reason for Failure is Greed

As a young teen, I had a positive feeling that I would one day become successful. I can even remember the exact spot where I was standing in the barnyard when I received the intuition. I had no idea how or when this would happen; all I knew was that someday it would. From that moment on, all I wanted was to be rich. I had dreamed of owning a vacation home, having fancy cars, and making lots of money. My obsession with making money caused me to make some bad investment choices later on in life. Greed became my idol and took complete control over me. However, my life did eventually turn around, once I eliminated greed from it. Greed happens to be one of the reasons why people fail in network marketing. A greedy person is unable to work as part of a team, leverage, or duplicate a system. They have no interest in helping others, only themselves. I won't go into much detail about my system, though; I've reserved that for the first edition of Cracking the Rich Code by Kevin Harrington and Jim Britt. There, I give a comprehensive explanation of how to apply the concepts of teamwork, leveraging, and duplication to build a large downline.

I will, however, share my creative stories, which I feel were largely responsible for my rise to success. My stories became an avenue for reaching out to others and promoting my concepts of teamwork, leveraging, and duplication as the only way to success. Stories are very effective, because they can be emotional and people can relate to them. They also tend to get stored in a person's long-term memory and are easier to recall. They're also efficient ways to brand yourself and create a following. I placed my stories on social sites and included summaries to reinforce the concept that teamwork, leveraging, and duplication were the only ways to achieve network-marketing success. I hope that you enjoy this information and the stories, and that they help you succeed in reaching your dreams.

The Lost Gold Nugget

Jack, a middle-aged man, prayed every day, asking God to give him financial help because he was struggling to feed his family. There were no jobs available, and he was buried deep in debt, borrowing from others. One night in a dream, God answered his prayer, telling Jack to climb the highest mountain behind his house and turn over the rock sitting at the very top of the mountain. Jack, being a man of faith, woke up full of excitement and told his wife about the dream. He hurried out to the shed, put on his hiking boots and headed up to the mountaintop. After three hours of intense climbing, he reached the very top of the mountain and noticed a large rock. He approached the rock, got down on all fours, and with all his remaining strength, rolled the rock over. Under it was a large gold nugget. Jack picked up the gold nugget and started jumping for joy. "Finally, my prayers have been answered," he said. So he placed the gold nugget in his pocket and rapidly started to descend down the mountain.

On his descent, Jack noticed many other rocks and decided to stop and look under them, hoping to find more gold nuggets. Before he knew it, he realized the sun was beginning to set, and he needed to get off the mountain before dark. He reached the bottom, where his family was waiting, and started yelling about the gold nugget he had found. Jack reached into his pocket to show them the gold nugget, but it wasn't there. He then realized that the nugget had fallen out of his pocket while he was searching for more. Jack returned to the mountaintop the next day in hopes of finding the lost gold nugget, but was unsuccessful. He continued searching for it every day for the rest of his life, but never did find it.

Author: Mark Recker 2018

Summary: Greed is one of the main reasons why people fail in network marketing. Zig Ziglar said, "If you help enough people get what they want, then you will get what you want." Unfortunately, greed does not allow for you to want to reach out to help others so that you can get what you want. If you want to be successful, then you need to work as part of a team, leverage, and duplicate a system.

It's Difficult to Change

One day, I received a phone call about an advertisement I had placed. I always let my calls go to voicemail, because it gives me a reason to call the person back to verify their information and FORM the prospect. FORM is an acronym for family, occupation, recreation, and message. I learned this many years ago in a sales class I was taking in college. It's a process that sales people will use to get to know their client better. I try to collect a prospect's name, mailing address, phone number, and email. In this case, I called the person and decided to really try to get to know him. When I asked him how things we're going, he said they were OK. So, I pressed him a little more intimately, and explained that a lot of people who call are really having a tough time with paying the bills. Then I asked him again if he was really doing OK. His tone changed this time, and he said he was going through some really difficult times and was looking for a way to earn some serious income. I told him that I completely understood, and explained that it's vital for a person to embrace CHANGE in their life before they can improve their situation. I then explained that the opportunity I was promoting offered a 30-day money back guarantee on the product. I also stated that I would cover the cost of shipping to return the product. That way, if my system did not earn him any income, he would pay nothing out of pocket. The very next words out of his mouth were that he could not afford the $36.95 to get started. I informed him that he had to be willing to embrace change and find the money if he wanted to really improve his situation. This person was not willing to embrace change! I find conversations like this are a great way to qualify a person so that you don't waste your time or money on a tire kicker.

Motivate Yourself with
Who, What, Where, When, and Why

There will be ups and downs along the way to success. If you find yourself becoming less motivated, then pick a nice quiet spot where you feel the most relaxed and go through the 5 Ws: who, what, where, when, and why.

Who am I, and what's my real purpose in life?

What do I want to accomplish for myself and others?

Where can I improve myself?

When can I expect to see results?

Why do I want this?

Overcoming Your Lack of Faith

One day a seedling from an oak tree became detached and was carried off by a strong gust of wind. The seedling became very scared, and cried out to God for help as it helplessly tumbled through the air. God heard its cry and calmed the wind to stop the seed from tumbling. The seed landed on a hard gravel surface and became afraid that a bird would swoop down and devour it. Once again the seedling cried out for help. God heard its cry again and sent a gentle wind to place the seedling in a shallow crevice and protect it from the birds.

Shortly after, the seedling became scared again when it became cold after the sun went down. God heard its cry and used the wind to coat the seed with a fine blanket of soil to keep it warm. The next day, the seed became scared when it became thirsty and dry after the sun rose. Once again, God answered its cry by gathering the rain clouds by sending it soft rain. The seedling then sprouted to life from the rain, and its fear was replaced by faith. It flourished and grew into a mighty oak tree offering shelter to all the creatures around it.

Author ~ Mark Recker 2018

Conclusion:

If you want to be successful in network marketing, you must have faith in teamwork, leveraging, and duplication. People only fail when they give up trying.

Weeping Willow Tree Solves Network Marketing Problem

A giant willow tree towered over all the other willows in her family. She was the mother of all willows surrounding her. Every day, she would stand watch over her sapling siblings and provide them wisdom on how to grow and mature into an adult willow tree. She was a wise old tree with a massive root system to hold her firmly in place.

One day, as she was providing wisdom to her family, a young and immature sapling yelled out to his mother, requesting faster growth. The sapling said, "Mother, I want to become tall and mighty like you, and I want it now." However, the mother willow tree, being the wisest, refused and said, "First, you need to learn my wisdom." However, the young sapling sibling became angry and intolerant towards his mother after he heard that. He refused to be patient and would no longer listen to his mother. Therefore, he started pushing aside his other brothers and sisters, stealing their sunlight and water so that he could grow faster than the rest.

Every day he would boast and brag about how tall he was growing, and show off his limbs to his family, flexing them in the gentle breeze. The sun would dance from his leaves and cast a dazzling brilliance upon him. While others in his family took notice and started to admire their brother, the mother grew sadder each day. When the willow tree finally reached the height of his mother he said, "Look at me, mother, I'm as tall as you and still growing faster than you!" "By next year, I will be the biggest in the forest and everyone will look up to me." The mother willow tree sadly looked aside and lowered her branches so that the tips of her branches touched the ground.

That night, a huge storm came by, with gale force winds blowing across the woods. As usual, the mother willow tree stretched out her branches and covered her sapling family to protect them. She could hear her son crying out for his mother in fear as he swayed from side to side. He started rocking back and forth to the point where his roots started leaving the ground below him. However, because he was so selfish and refused his mother's wisdom, his roots were set very shallowly and could not support his height. When morning came, the son laid on the ground, with his mother standing next to him, weeping. Hence, the name "weeping willow tree" came to be known.

Author: Mark Recker 2018

Conclusion:

Network marketing requires a lot of patience. Too many people are in a fast and furious push to market their opportunity without learning the proper steps to build relationships with their potential business partners. When they don't see immediate progress, they often jump into another opportunity and repeat the same mistakes over and over. In order to be successful, you must learn how to work as part of a team, leverage, duplicate, and have patience.

Can Technology Make You Wealthy?

There is no doubt that technology has made our lives easier. In manufacturing, the use of robots has increased production output and decreased labor costs. Today, you don't have to go house to house or meet at a coffee shop to show others your opportunity. There is no shortage of network marketing technology for sending out solo ads, email blasts, and pay-per-click advertising to thousands of prospects at the click of a mouse. Landing and capture pages are working 24 hours a day, 7 days a week, providing you a sales funnel. Those who respond back with their email addresses are fed into an email auto-responder with enticing scripts to convince them to join.

The Change[16]

With all these technological advances making money online has never been easier¾or has it? Who's really making the money here?

The 3 Fishermen

There were three friends who were laid off from work and behind on all their bills. They were sitting around one day reading the newspaper, looking for job openings. The economy was the worst ever since the Great Depression, and jobs were scarce. While looking at the help ads, they noticed an advertisement for a fishing tournament that was paying a $5000.00 prize for the largest fish caught.

The entry fee was only $100.00 per person, so they decided to share an old boat that they borrowed from a friend.

All three friends were determined to win because they all needed the money and were way behind on bills. Tom visited a bait shop and saw a high-tech lure that had sonar technology that would target only large fish. It was the only one in the store and had a price tag of $500.00. He decided that the cost was justified, and the salesman really bragged about how well it worked. So he handed over his credit card and maxed it out to purchase this lure.

Bill visited another bait shop and saw a high-tech fishing lure that had state-of-the-art radar-seeking capabilities and targeted only large fish. The salesman bragged about how good the reviews were, and convinced Bill to purchase it for the asking price of $500.00. He too, pulled out his credit card and maxed it out in hopes of winning the fishing tournament.

On the morning of the tournament, Mark grabbed an old tin can and shovel and dug up the nicest-looking earthworms he could find.

All three friends got inside the borrowed boat and started on their way to their favorite fishing spot. They all threw in their lines in anticipation of catching the biggest fish. Tom felt a big tug on his line and jerked back on the rod. His rod was bent almost to the breaking point and he was fighting to reel in his catch. Bill also felt a tug and jerked back on his rod, bending it almost to breaking point while reeling it in. Mark also felt a tug and jerked back on his rod, bending it moderately. When Tom finally got his rod reeled in, he noticed a large rubber boot attached to the lure and the lure broken in half. When Bill got his rod reeled in, he noticed a pair of waders attached to his lure, which was also broken. Mark reeled in his catch, pulling in a huge large-mouth bass and winning the tournament.

Author ~ Mark Recker 2018

Summary: People join others they like and trust, and you only work with the willing. This requires that you talk to people and offer to help them to become successful. You have to work as part of a team, leverage, and duplicate in order to be successful. Investing in leads, solo ads, landing pages, and other types of automated tools will not guarantee you success. Network marketing is all about developing friendships and offering help.

Motivation Creates Determination

Motivation is usually brought on by a need that has to be met. It can be an emotional need or a practical need, such as money. Many refer to this as their WHY. If your WHY or motivation is big enough, then your determination will fulfill it. Below is a story I wrote about three wise men who were challenged by the king. I used this story to promote the health and wellness opportunity that I'm currently involved with. In all my stories, I created links back to my team website to increase search engine rankings.

I saved my most popular story for the first release of Cracking the Rich Code by Kevin Harrington and Jim Britt. I hope that you will purchase it and also learn how to implement teamwork, leveraging, and duplication, to grow the business that you're involved with.

Which is More Important, Your Health or Your Wealth?

The Change[16]

Three wise men were imprisoned for life by the king for giving out improper advice. He was nearing the end of his life, and decided to offer a pardon to the wise man who could answer life's most important question, which only he knew the answer to. He had his soldiers round up the imprisoned wise men and bring them to his throne.

The king said that he would pardon the wise men if they could answer the question correctly. One by one, the palace guards brought the three wise men in front of the king. So the king asked the first wise man, "Which is more important, your health or your wealth?" The first wise man quickly answered, "Your health!" The king stared at the wise man for a moment and said, "Your pardon is denied." The king ordered his guards to bring in the second wise man and asked him, "What is more important, your health or your wealth?" The wise man immediately yelled out, "Your wealth!" The king stared at the wise man for a while and said, "Your pardon is denied."

The king then ordered the palace guards to bring forward the third wise man, and asked the same question: "Which is more important, your health or your wealth?" The wise man stood in silence for a few moments, and then he said, "Your Majesty, both are equally important." The king then asked him to explain his answer.

The wise man went on to say that without health you have nothing to live for. You can't be pain free and enjoy life the way you want to. However, without wealth you will worry about how you are going to make ends meet and then stress overtakes your body and disease sets in. You need a balance of wealth and health to live a long, healthy life. One without the other is meaningless.

"Perfect answer," said the king, and he pardoned the wise man and returned him to his original position as the king's main wise man.

***

To contact Mark:

cell: 260-804-4084

www.markrecker.com

office: 260-625-4084

email: mrecker777@gmail.com

Team Website: www.JDILifeTeam.com

Facebook Page: https://www.facebook.com/groups/TrueGlobalCompassion

AFTERWORD

Life is always a series of transitions… people, places, and things that shape who we are as individuals. Often, you never know that the next catalyst for change is around the corner.

Jim Britt and Jim Lutes have spent decades influencing individuals to blossom into the best version of themselves.

Allow all you have read in this book to create introspection and redirection if required. It's your journey to craft.

The Change is a series. A global movement. Watch for future releases and add them to your collection. If you know of anyone who would like to be considered as a co-author for a future book, have them email our offices at support@jimbritt.com.

The individual and combined works of Jim Britt and Jim Lutes have filled seminar rooms to maximum capacity and created a worldwide demand.

The blessings go both ways, as Jim and Jim are always willing students of life. Out of demand for life-changing programs and events, Jim and Jim conduct seminars and keynote presentations worldwide.

To Schedule Jim Britt or Jim Lutes as your featured speaker at your next convention or special event, or to organize and host a seminar in your area, email: support@jimbritt.com

Master your moment as they become hours that become days.

Your legacy awaits.

All the best,

Jim Britt and Jim Lutes

www.JimBritt.com

www.LutesInternational.com

www.ingramcontent.com/pod-product-compliance
Lightning Source LLC
Chambersburg PA
CBHW070052080526
44586CB00013B/1028